D0379981

THE DEVOTIONAL LIBRARY

GENERAL EDITORS: PROFESSOR JAMES B TORRANCE
AND DR MICHAEL JINKINS

JOHN KNOX

JOHN KNOX

AN ACCOUNT OF THE DEVELOPMENT
OF HIS SPIRITUALITY

Dr Henry R Sefton

THE DEVOTIONAL LIBRARY

SAINT ANDREW PRESS
EDINBURGH

First published in 1993 by
SAINT ANDREW PRESS
121 George Street, Edinburgh EH2 4YN

Copyright © Dr Henry R Sefton 1993
Reprinted 2000

ISBN 0 7152 0663 X

All rights reserved. No part of this publication may be reproduced or
transmitted in any form or by any means, electronic or mechanical,
including photocopy, recording, or information storage and retrieval
system, without permission in writing from the publisher. This book is
sold, subject to the condition that it shall not, by way of trade or
otherwise, be lent, re-sold, hired out or otherwise circulated without the
publisher's prior consent.

British Library Cataloguing in Publication Data

A catalogue record for this book
is available from the British Library.

ISBN 071520663X

This book has been set in 12/13 pt Garamond.

Printed and bound by Redwood Books, Trowbridge.

CONTENTS

JOHN KNOX
Part 1
Knox the Man

JOHN KNOX
Part 2
Extracts from Knox's Writings

GENERAL EDITORS' FOREWORD

MOST of us have heard the names of the great theologians. Perhaps we are even familiar with their theological writings. What goes frequently unrecognised, however, is the spiritual depth, the rich devotional thought. The great theologians were first and foremost persons of faith, persons with a great deal to offer us.

In a time when bookshops present us with a startling array of devotional resources that sometimes provide rather less than advertised, we feel that it would be valuable to dig a bit deeper into some richer veins. Our guides for this trek will be, themselves, scholars intimately familiar with the great theologians and appreciative of the spiritual life of the Christian. They will take us into the depths of the devotional thought of these theologians with sensitivity and care.

The goal of The Devotional Library is to provide a collection of the finest devotional thought available, in a set of readable, attractive and affordable books. The first three in our series will introduce the devotional thought of *John Knox* (ed. Dr Henry Sefton), *Thomas Erskine* (by Dr Trevor Hart) and *John McLeod Campbell* (Dr Michael Jinkins). Other books to follow will introduce us to Henry Scougal, George MacDonald, James S Stewart, P T Forsyth, and others. Our prayer is that The Devotional Library will provide ministers and laypersons with a vast resource of the finest devotional literature in the English language, so that we learn the devotional life from people whose lives have been remarkable for their depth.

GENERAL EDITORS
Reverend Professor James B Torrance
Reverend Dr Michael Jinkins

Author's Preface

The Aim of this Book

THERE have been so many biographies of John Knox that some reason has to be given for providing another book about him. The aim of this book is to let John Knox speak, as far as possible, for himself and to show how the circumstances of his life shaped the style of his spirituality.

The intention is to do for our day what the Reverend Thomas Thomson did in 1845 when he prepared *Select Practical Writings of John Knox* for a committee of the General Assembly of the Free Church of Scotland.

I am grateful to the Reverend Dr Michael Jinkins for the invitation to prepare this contribution to the Devotional Library and to Miss Lesley Taylor and her staff at Saint Andrew Press for much patience and kindness.

I should like to dedicate this small book to the Reverend Professor James S McEwen DD, master interpreter of John Knox, with respect and affection.

Henry R Sefton
ABERDEEN

JOHN KNOX
Part 1: Knox the Man

KNOX'S EARLY LIFE

LIKE many of his fellow-countrymen John Knox was remarkably reticent. Thus, although he is one of the most famous Scotsmen of all time, we know surprisingly little about the man himself—the private John Knox. This ignorance extends even to the date and place of his birth. Until comparatively recently he was thought to have been born in 1505 and there were quater-centenary celebrations of the event in 1905. Now it is generally agreed that he was born about 1514. Similarly Gifford in East Lothian has been claimed as his birthplace, but it is more likely that he was born in Giffordgate on the outskirts of Haddington.

The Knox family seem to have been of no great importance, although his father, a yeoman farmer, was prosperous enough to set up his eldest son William in business and to give his son John a good education. There is no documentary evidence about where he received that education, but George Buchanan states that Knox attended St Andrews University during the time that John Major was teaching there. This John Major had made a name for himself during his time at Paris as a distinguished and acute critic of the existing ecclesiastical regime. The influence of such a man on the young John Knox must have been considerable. Despite this, Knox seems to have sought a career in the service of the existing Church.

A reference to 'Sir John Knox' in 1540 does not mean

that Knox had been knighted, but indicates that by then he had been ordained as a priest. He was also a papal notary which meant that he could authenticate legal documents and prepare various kinds of ecclesiastical papers. The last document which Knox prepared is dated 27 March 1543 and bears an attestation in an unusual form: *Testis per Christum fidelis cui gloria* ('The faithful witness through Christ, to whom be the glory'). It has been suggested that this means that Knox had by then become a Protestant.

Knox himself tells us nothing directly about his conversion. The historian, David Calderwood, who was almost a contemporary of Knox, asserts that Thomas Gwilliam, a Dominican or Black Friar 'was the first man from whom Mr Knox received any taste of the truth.' Gwilliam belonged to Athelstaneford, which is only three miles from Haddington and so it is possible that he and Knox knew each other quite well.[1]

Another account comes from Richard Bannatyne, Knox's secretary during the Reformer's last years. Bannatyne says that Knox on his death bed asked that the seventeenth chapter of St John's Gospel should be read, for it was there, he said, 'I cast my first anchor.' This seems to indicate that Knox's conversion was not something into which he drifted, but was the result of a definite decision at which he arrived on the basis of what he read in John 17.[2] It may well be significant that Knox's most considerable theological treatise has an eloquent commentary on the High Priestly Prayer of Christ in that chapter (Extract I, p 42).

Some time in 1543 Knox became the tutor for the two sons of Hugh Douglas of Longniddry and the son of John Cockburn of Ormiston and took up residence at Longniddry, on the coast between Leith and Haddington. This meant that he was associated with a group of lairds who were pro-Protestant and pro-England. Knox does not say why he made this move, but it seems to indicate that he was now firmly committed to the Protestant cause.

The following year Knox made his adherence to the reforming cause public when he accompanied the Protestant preacher George Wishart as his bodyguard, carrying a two-handed sword during Wishart's preaching tour of Lothian. It would seem that Knox attached considerable importance to this public appearance for it is the first occasion he mentions himself in his *History of the Reformation in Scotland.* When Wishart's liberty and life seemed to be in danger from the civil and ecclesiastical authorities, Knox was anxious to continue with him; but Wishart replied, 'Nay return to your bairns, and God bless you. One is sufficient for a sacrifice.' Wishart's premonition was fulfilled when he was condemned as a heretic and burnt at the stake on 1 March 1546 outside the Castle of St Andrews, while the Cardinal Archbishop David Beaton watched from a window in the castle.

Later that year on 29 May the Castle of St Andrews was invaded by friends of Wishart. They broke into the Cardinal's room, rebuked him for his part in Wishart's execution and stabbed him to death. For more than a year the Castilians, as they came to be known, remained in occupation of the castle. Two of them were the fathers of Knox's pupils and at Easter 1547 the boys and Knox came to St Andrews where it was thought they would be safer. There the lessons were continued including, Knox tells us, the exposition of the Gospel according to John.

Once again the Fourth Gospel appears to have played an important part in the spiritual development of John Knox. His instruction of his pupils on the Gospel was overheard and from then on Knox had no peace until he consented to become a preacher (Extract II, p 45). John Rough, the chaplain

to the garrison in the Castle, preached a sermon on the
election of ministers and when he had finished, he directed a
personal appeal to Knox to accept a call to the preaching
ministry. Knox's immediate response was to burst into tears
and to refuse to say yea or nay.

It was not long before Knox was driven to decide. When
attending a debate between John Rough and John Annand,
Dean of the Cathedral, Knox intervened to say that he could
prove that the Church of Rome was 'further degenerate from
the purity which was in the days of the Apostles than was
the Church of the Jews from the ordinance given by Moses,
when they consented to the innocent death of Christ.' Not
surprisingly of course, Knox was challenged to make good
his words.

Knox seems to have regarded this challenge as a confirmation of his call to be a preacher of the Gospel. This
gave him the confidence to preach a sermon which made a
powerful impact on those who heard it. In his *History of the
Reformation in Scotland,* Knox reports these comments on his
sermon: 'Others sned the branches of the Papistry, but he
strikes at the root, to destroy the whole' and 'Master George
Wishart spake ever so plainly, and yet he was burnt: even
so will he be' (Extract III, p 47).

No doubt Knox was proud of the comparison with George
Wishart and there was at least the possibility that he would
suffer a similar fate when the castle was taken by the Regent,
the Earl of Arran, with French help in July 1547. However,
the Castilians' lives were spared. The gentry were impris-
oned in France, while the rest—including Knox—were sent
to row in the galleys of the French fleet.

Some years later, in a letter to Mrs Anna Locke which
was written from St Andrews, Knox refers to the torments of
those galleys over the space of nineteen months, and adds:

'Then was I assuredly persuaded, that I should not die till I had preached Christ Jesus, even where I now am.'[3]

There must have been times during Knox's service in the galleys when he had some leisure, for he wrote a summary of a work by his friend Henry Balnaves on Justification. He managed to smuggle it back to Scotland with an accompanying letter to 'his best beloved Brethren of the Congregation of the Castle of St Andrews.' Knox later commented that this Summary contained 'the sum of his doctrine and confession of his faith' (Extract IV, p 49 and Extract V, p 52).

KNOX IN ENGLAND

KNOX was released from the French galleys in March 1549 probably due to the intervention of the government of King Edward VI of England, which was pushing forward the Protestant reformation there. Knox was licensed to preach by the English Privy Council and sent to commend the reformed faith in Berwick, a town full of English soldiers returning from the raids in Scotland, and refugees from Scotland and its pro-French government. A further problem was that the bishop of the diocese, Bishop Tunstall of Durham, was not sympathetic to reform and the Prayer Book of 1549 was therefore unknown in the north of England. Knox turned this situation to his own advantage by devising an order of service much simpler than those of the Prayer Book and giving much more prominence to the sermon.

Knox's time in Berwick was of great importance in his development as a preacher and pastor. Addressing a congregation which included many soldiers, he developed the use of terms of war and conflict in his sermons especially when attacking 'the idolatry of the mass.' He thought of himself as a kind of Joshua blowing trumpets around the walls of a modern Jericho. He would preach a series of sermons on a doctrinal subject—such as prayer—or else he preached through a book of the Bible, verse by verse. He would begin with an exposition of the verse or passage in order to show that he was preaching God's Word. Then he would draw out the doctrinal implications of the text contrasting true and false doctrine. Finally he would close with an application of both text and doctrine to the particular circumstances of those who heard him. These pointed observations on the contemporary situation were to land Knox in trouble from his time in Berwick to the end of his life.

Knox was equally insistent that the sacraments should be properly administered. The absolute rule in this was the New Testament and particularly the commands and example of Christ. A fragmentary manuscript[4] gives us an outline of the practice of the Lord's Supper used in Berwick-upon-Tweed by John Knox. After preaching sermons on the benefits of God given to us by Jesus Christ, based on chapters 13 to 16 of St John's Gospel, he offered a prayer for faith. This was followed by the reading of 1 Corinthians 11:17-31: 'Then must be declared what persons be unworthy to be partakers thereof; and because no flesh is just in the sight of God, common prayer shall be made in form of confession.' A specimen prayer of confession is given in the manuscript after which the minister is to read 'some notable place of the Evangel wherein God's mercy is most evidently declared' to assure the penitent of full remission of all offences. After praying for the congregation, the minister distributed the bread and wine to communicants seated at tables. There also survives from this period a summary written by Knox on the Sacrament of the Lord's Supper according to the Holy Scriptures (Extract VI, p 55).

Because of his attacks on the 'Mass' (a term which was still used in the English Prayer Book of 1549) Knox was summoned to appear before the Council of the North. Normally such interviews took place in private, but Knox was instructed to give his defence before a large congregation in the parish church of Newcastle on 4 April 1550. At the beginning of his *Vindication of the Doctrine that the Mass is idolatry*, Knox acknowledges the important place that the

Mass had occupied in the religious life of his hearers:

> I know that in the Mass hath not only been esteemed great
> holiness and honouring of God, but also the ground and
> foundation of our religion. So that, in opinion of many,
> the Mass taken away, there resteth no true worshipping
> nor honouring of God in the earth.[5]

The importance of the Mass derived from the fact that it
was thought to occupy 'the place of the last and mystical
Supper of our Lord Jesus.' Knox's aim was to prove that
instead it was 'Idolatry before God, and blasphemous to the
Death and Passion of Christ, and contrary to the Supper of
Jesus Christ.' To do this he set out some propositions:

> All worshipping, honouring, or service invented by the
> brain of man in the religion of God, without His own
> express commandment is Idolatry. The Mass is invented
> by the brain of man, without any commandment of God:
> Therefore it is Idolatry.

> All honouring or service of God, whereunto is added a
> wicked opinion, is abomination. Unto the Mass is added a
> wicked opinion. Therefore it is abomination.[6]

Knox's principal argument was an attack on the doctrine
of 'the sacrifice of the altar': 'If ye offer Christ in sacrifice for
sin, ye shed his blood, and thus newly slay him.' But he bids
them not to be afraid, 'for Jesus Christ may suffer no more,
shed his blood no more, nor die no more.'

The term 'Mass' was dropped from the English Prayer
Book when it was revised in 1552, but Knox was unhappy
about the rubric which directed communicants to kneel

when receiving the Bread and Wine. He insisted on a comment being added that this direction was not to be taken as implying 'that any adoration is done or ought to be done either unto the Sacramental bread or wine there bodily received or unto any real and essential presence there being of Christ's natural flesh and blood.' This is popularly known as the Black Rubric because it was printed in black instead of the more usual red (Extract VII, p 58, Extract VIII, p 60).

Knox's congregation at Berwick were not all soldiers. One of the most prominent of the civilians was Elizabeth Bowes of Aske, the wife of the captain of nearby Norham Castle. Mrs Bowes had probably become a Protestant prior to Knox's arrival in Berwick, but her husband Richard had not; and of her fifteen children, only two of them, Marjory and George, shared her faith. Mrs Bowes was a woman of strong convictions who at times encouraged Knox when he was depressed. However, on the other hand, she had continual doubts and fears about her own spiritual condition. Did she have true faith? Was she one of the elect? Had she committed the unpardonable sin? Those uncertainties caused her constantly to consult Knox. When he was not available for personal consultation she wrote to him. Many of the letters he wrote in reply have been preserved and give us a good insight into Knox's pastoral care (Extract X, p 65).

The letters are an impressive mixture of Scriptural principles and down-to-earth commonsense. 'Remember, Sister,' he tells her, 'that the tempter departed from Christ only for a time, and therefore be not discouraged, albeit he return to you with new and deceitful assaults.' Certainly the Devil is a roaring lion seeking whom he may devour, but those 'whom he has devoured already he seeks no more.' Her very fears are proof that she is a Christian. If she had none, something would be wrong.'

The needs of Mrs Bowes and her like at Berwick may have been the mainspring for another piece of work completed by Knox about this time. This was *A Declaration what true Prayer is, how we should pray and for what we should pray* (Extract XI, p 68).

In 1551 Knox was moved to Newcastle and later that year was appointed one of the King's six chaplains. This latter appointment involved not only preaching before the young king, Edward VI, but also travelling to commend the cause of Reformation. He was later offered, but refused, the bishopric of Rochester and the rich living of All Hallows, Bread Street in London. His reasons for refusal were a reluctance to use the Prayer Book which he had been able to ignore in his ministry in the north of England and an anxiety about the shape of things to come after the death of the frail young king.

Edward VI died on 6 July 1553, aged only sixteen. Knox saw the king's death as a judgment on the nation:

> Omnipotent and everlasting God, Father of our Lord Jesus Christ, who by thy eternal providence disposes kingdoms as best seemeth to thy wisdom: we acknowledge and confess thy judgments to be righteous, in that thou hast taken from us, for our ingratitude, and for abusing of thy most holy word, our Native King and earthly comforter.[8]

Knox then goes on to pray for the new Queen, Mary Tudor:

> Illuminate the heart of our Sovereign Lady Queen Mary with pregnant gifts of the Holy Ghost. And inflame the hearts of her Council with thy true fear and love. Repress thou the pride of those that would rebel; and remove

from all hearts the contempt of the Word. Let not our
enemies rejoice at our destruction, but look thou to the
honour of thy own name, O Lord; and let thy Gospel be
preached with boldness in this Realm.[9]

Knox made use of the brief months of toleration at the
beginning of Mary Tudor's reign to preach with boldness the
perils which would befall England if it were to return to
Papistry. In a letter to Mrs Bowes dated 20 September 1553
he tells her that he has been so occupied with his labours in
Kent that he has not been able to give much thought to the
'process' between herself and her husband over his marriage
to their daughter Marjory! It was becoming clear that
Knox's continuance in England was a risk both to himself
and his friends and so he crossed to Dieppe in France sometime in January 1554.

England had been good *for* Knox and good *to* Knox; and
just before he left, he wrote these words:

Sometime I have thought that impossible it had been,
so to have removed my affection from the Realm of
Scotland, that any Realm or Nation could have been
equal dear unto me. But God I take to record in my conscience, that the troubles present (and appearing to be)
in the Realm of England, are double more dolorous unto
my heart, than ever were the troubles of Scotland.[10]

KNOX ON THE CONTINENT

SINCE he could no longer preach to his flocks in England, Knox wrote *A Godly Letter of Warning or Admonition to the faithful in London, Newcastle and Berwick.* Two editions of the *Godly Letter* were printed in 1554. The second bore the fictitious statement, 'Imprinted in Rome before the Castel of S. Aungel at the signe of Sainct Peter'—which suggests a wry sense of humour on the part of either Knox or his printer. But there is nothing humorous about the *Godly Letter.* Knox is appalled at what is happening in England under the reign of the Catholic Mary Tudor and he urges the faithful to refuse to participate in the idolatry of the Mass (Extract XIII, p 74).

The developing situation in England, in which it seemed to Knox that the enemies to God's truth were triumphing, caused him to meditate on the sixth Psalm and to write a lengthy exposition of it. Some of it was written before he left England, but it was completed during his stay in Dieppe and dispatched from there. There are several very personal reflections in the Exposition:

> What moved me to refuse, and that with displeasure, of all men, (even of those that best loved me), those high promotions that were offered, by him whom God hath taken from us for our offences? Assuredly the foresight of trouble to come. How oft have I said unto you, that the time would not be long, that England would give me bread?[11]

Knox is not sure why he fled England, but he *is* sure that the fear of death was not the main cause; and although he has seemed to play the faint-hearted and feeble soldier, he is anxious to be restored to the battle again.[12] He remains convinced that the doctrine which he and his associates had preached in England is the only Word of Life.

But Knox is not just concerned to exhort and encourage the faithful. He is also very anxious to have some guidance from some of the leading Reformers on the question of obedience to a magistrate who enforces idolatry and condemns true religion. So in March 1554 he went to Geneva to consult John Calvin, who referred him to Pierre Viret in Lausanne and Henry Bullinger in Zurich. Bullinger's answers, with which Calvin agreed, have been preserved. They cannot have helped Knox very much, for Bullinger concludes:

There is need, therefore, in cases of this kind, of much prayer, and much wisdom, lest by precipitancy and corrupt affections we should so act as to occasion mischief to many worthy persons.[13]

Knox returned to Dieppe where he learned that the English bishops who had favoured Protestantism were either in prison or under house arrest and that many prominent lay people had returned to the old ways of worship. However there were many who were meeting in secret for prayer, Bible study and mutual exhortation. For their benefit he wrote *Two Comfortable Epistles to his Afflicted Brethren in England*. He refers to his travels and his discussions with the Swiss Reformers and makes the significant statement: 'But hereof be assured, that all is not lawful nor just that is statute by Civil Laws, neither yet is everything sin before God whilk ungodly persons allege to be treason.'[14] Here is a

hint that 'lawful' might be defined in such a way as to justify
resistance to authority.

In July 1554 Knox published a longer and much more
vigorous pamphlet entitled *A Faithful Admonition to the Professors
of God's Truth in England.* The pamphlet is on the one hand an
elaborate exposition of the Biblical accounts of the incidents
leading up to Christ walking on the water; and on the other
a vehement denunciation of Queen Mary and her ministers,
and her allies Emperor Charles V and Philip of Spain. He
even regrets that Mary and Bishop Gardiner had not been
executed as they deserved to be for their idolatry. He also
makes an attack on rule by a woman: 'But the saying is too
true, that the usurped government of an affectionate [*ie*
emotional] woman is a rage without reason.'[15] There is also
an interesting discussion on the duty of a preacher and
reflections on the part he and his fellow preachers had played
in the closing months of Edward's reign (Extract XIV, p 77).

In August 1554 Knox left Dieppe for Geneva where he
hoped to study under the guidance of some of the leading
Reformers. His studies were interrupted in November 1554
by a call from Frankfurt to come and minister to a congregation of English exiles in that city—a call which, somewhat
reluctantly, and under pressure from Calvin, he accepted.
There he immediately found himself in the midst of a con-
troversy over the use of the Second Book of Common Prayer,
a book about which he had considerable reservations.

The Frankfurt congregation was split between a vociferous
minority who regarded the use of the Prayer Book as essential and a majority which was happy with a much simpler
order of worship prepared by a young layman called William
Whittingham. The minority received considerable support
from English exiles elsewhere, particularly in Strasbourg.
Knox refused to use the Prayer Book and suggested that he

should confine himself to preaching while another minister led the worship. This was rejected. Two new orders of worship were prepared. The first was prepared by Knox and Whittingham and three other English 'radicals'. This was immediately rejected by the 'conservative' group and a second order, which was a simplified version of the Prayer Book services, was compiled as a 'Liturgy of Compromise'. This compromise liturgy omitted the responses said by the congregation and was used with a fair degree of harmony for just over a month. The harmony was shattered when a new arrival called Richard Cox insisted on saying the responses in a loud voice. Within a fortnight Knox was ousted by Cox and the magistrates of Frankfort expelled him from the city because of the seditious remarks he had made about the Emperor Charles V in the *Faithful Admonition*.

It was of course less than tactful of Knox to refer to the Emperor as 'no less enemy unto Christ than ever was Nero', but his reaction to the news of his expulsion was to preach a sermon on the text 'He is not Caesar's friend'. The next day he set out for Geneva. There he hoped to resume his studies, but he found it difficult to settle down and after four months, he returned to Scotland.

KNOX IN SCOTLAND 1555-56

WITH characteristic reticence Knox does not tell us why he returned to Scotland in 1555, but in a letter to Mrs Bowes he wrote:

Albeit my journey toward Scotland, beloved mother, was maist contrarious to my own judgment, before I did enterprise the same, yet this day I praise God for them wha was the cause external of my resort to these quarters; that is, I praise God in you and for you, whom he made the instrument to draw me from the den of my own ease (you alone did draw me from the rest of quiet study) to contemplate and behold the fervent thirst of our brethren, night and day sobbing and groaning for the bread of life. If I had not seen it with my eyes in my own country, I could not have believed it.[16]

In spite of what Knox says in this letter, Mrs Bowes may well have had another matter in mind in urging Knox to return: the 'process' (as he had called it) over his marriage to her daughter Marjory! Shortly after this, Knox wrote almost apologetically to Mrs Bowes:

Albeit I was fully purposed to have visited you before this time, yet hath God laid impediments which I could not avoid: they are such as I doubt not are to his glory and to the comfort of many here.[17]

The exact date of Knox's marriage to Marjory Bowes is not known. Many years later, in 1572, Knox published a letter which he had written to Mrs Bowes in July 1554 and gave this explanation why he addressed her as mother in that letter:

> I had made a faithful promise, before witness, to Marjory Bowes her daughter; and so as she took me for son, I heartily embraced her as my mother.[18]

This probably does not refer to a marriage, but to a binding engagement known in English law as a precontract. It is likely that the actual marriage took place in Edinburgh some time in 1555 or 1556.

Knox's correspondence with Mrs Bowes indicates that he had been both surprised and delighted with the progress that the cause of Reformation had made in Scotland. In particular he mentions three wonderful days in Edinburgh: 'The trumpet blew the auld sound three days together, till private houses of indifferent largeness could not contain the voice of it.'[19] He also went on a preaching mission which covered most of central Scotland and reached as far north as Dun, near Montrose, where he was the guest of the laird, John Erskine.

During what proved to be a short visit, a turning point was reached in the Reformation movement in Scotland. Knox was appalled that many who favoured reform were continuing to attend Mass. John Erskine of Dun called a supper-meeting with several of the leaders of the Protestant party when the question was very thoroughly discussed. It was pointed out that even the Apostle Paul 'at the commandment of James and of the elders of Jerusalem passed to the temple and feigned himself to pay his vow with others'

(Acts 21:18-33). Knox's reply was that Paul's conduct had nothing to do with their going to Mass. To pay vows was sometimes God's command, but never idolatry. The Mass was, and always had been, idolatry. Furthermore, said Knox, Paul's compliance with James' wishes had been followed by disastrous consequences.

The discussion was ended by William Maitland of Lethington admitting on behalf of the others: 'I see perfectly, that our shifts will serve nothing before God, seeing that they stand us in so small stead before man.'[20] Because they had ceased to attend Mass, Knox celebrated the Lord's Supper in several of the country mansions of the leading reform sympathisers.

These activities inevitably attracted the notice of the existing ecclesiastical authorities and Knox was summoned to appear before the Bishops of Scotland in Edinburgh on 15 May 1556. When Knox arrived at the city with Erskine of Dun and several other gentlemen and nobles, the Bishops dropped the case. Instead of appearing before the Bishops on 15 May, Knox preached to a larger congregation than ever before in Edinburgh. An Edinburgh merchant called Thomas Marjoribanks gave him the use of a property known as the Bishop of Dunkeld's tenement on the north side of the High Street in Edinburgh and for ten days Knox preached to large audiences both morning and afternoon. The sermon on the first temptation of Christ, later published in London, was probably preached at this time (Extract XV, p 79).

A number of the nobles, hoping to influence the new Regent, the Queen Mother Mary of Guise, asked Knox to write her a letter to persuade her to reform the Church. This he did in terms of almost grovelling politeness:

Superfluous and foolish it shall appear to many that I,

a man of base estate and condition, dare enterprise to admonish a Princess so honourable, endowed with wisdom and graces singularly. But when I consider the honour that God commandeth to be given to Magistrates, which, no doubt, if it be true honour, containeth in itself, in lawful things obedience, and in all things love and reverence; when, further, I consider the troublesome estate of Christ Jesus' true religion, this day oppressed by blindness of men ... I am compelled to say that unless in your regiment [*ie* rule] and using of power, your Grace be found different from the multitude of Princes and head rulers, that this pre-eminence wherein ye are placed shall be your dejection to torment and pain everlasting.[21]

Knox told the Regent that it would be his duty to warn her if she were about to drink from a cup which he knew to be poisoned and so he warns her that:

The religion which this day men defend by fire and sword is a cup envenomed, of which whosoever drinketh, (except, by true repentance, he after drink of the water of life), drinketh therewith damnation and death.[22]

The Magistrates (by which he means rulers) have a duty to discipline false bishops as well as false judges. Knox recognises that all superstition cannot be abolished at once, nor all unprofitable pastors removed from office—but he urges her to study 'how that the true worshipping of God may be promoted.' Mary of Guise was not impressed and she handed Knox's letter to the Archbishop of Glasgow saying, 'Please you, my Lord, to read a *pasquil* [*ie* lampoon].'[23]

Six weeks after writing his letter to the Regent, Knox left Scotland and, after joining his wife and mother-in-law at

Dieppe, returned to Geneva. Why this sudden departure when all seemed to be going well in Scotland? In his *History of the Reformation in Scotland* Knox says that he was commanded in God's name to return to Geneva to care for the English Kirk which included those who had left Frankfurt with him in 1555. But there are hints that he foresaw troubles to come in Scotland not unlike those in England. In a letter from Geneva to some women members of the Protestant group in Edinburgh, Knox wrote:

> Shall Christ, the author of peace, concord and quietness, be preached where war is proclaimed, sedition engendered and tumults appear to rise? Shall not his Evangel be accused, as the cause of all calamity which is like to follow?[24]

And so he said to himself:

> What joy shall it be to thy heart to behold with thy eyes thy native country betrayed in the hands of strangers, whilk to nae man's judgment can be avoided, because that they wha ought to defend it, and the liberty thereof, are sae blind, dull and obstinate, that they will not see their own destruction?[25]

It seems that Knox saw the immediate future of the Reformed Faith in Scotland in terms of house-churches or 'privy kirks', and so he wrote for them *A Most Wholesome Counsel how to behave ourselves in the midst of this Wicked Generation,* in which he gave detailed advice about reading and study of Scripture and family and corporate worship (Extract XVI, p 81, Extract XVII, p 84 and Extract XVIII, p 87).

KNOX IN GENEVA AND DIEPPE 1556-59

ONE has the impression that Knox hoped to settle in Geneva. His sons, Nathaniel and Eleazar, were born there. But in 1557 he was invited to return to Scotland, very shortly after Nathaniel's birth, and rather reluctantly he set out and reached as far as Dieppe where he found another letter suggesting that the time was not ripe for his return.

During the winter of 1557-8 he remained at Dieppe, hoping for a change in the situation in Scotland, but also busy on his most famous work *The First Blast of the Trumpet against the Monstrous Regiment of Women*. Like other contemporary writers, Knox considered that women should not rule. He also thought that most of the problems faced by true believers in Scotland, France and England were caused by women usurping the authority which should be exercised by men (Extract XIX, p 89, Extract XX, p 92).

Back in Geneva in the spring of 1558, he became a burgess of the city and settled down to his pastoral duties and to an extensive programme of writing and publishing. It was now that he worked out his theory of a 'godly revolution'. A subject must normally obey a lawful ruler, but a time may come when because of the unlawful demands of the ruler the subject must disobey even to the point of armed resistance. In pursuit of this theory Knox re-issued his letter to the Queen Mother Regent of Scotland. He wrote to the nobles of Scotland telling them that they had a duty to suppress idolatry and establish true religion, even against the wishes of the monarch. Since he did not entirely trust the

nobles, he also wrote to the 'Commonalty of Scotland', point-
ing out that they had a right and a duty to demand reform
(Extract XXI, p 94).

In addition to these pamphlets, Knox was taking part
in the translation and annotation of the English version of
the Scriptures known as the Geneva Bible, conducting an
extensive correspondence and also writing a massive treatise
on Predestination (Extract I, p 42, Extract XXII, p 97 and
Extract XXIII, p 99). Knox was obviously very happy in
Geneva and he makes this very clear in a letter to his friend
Mrs Locke in London:

> In my heart I would have wished, yea and can not cease
> to wish, that it would please God to guide and conduct
> your self to this place, where I neither fear nor shame to
> say is the most perfect school of Christ that ever was in
> the earth since the days of the Apostles. In other places, I
> confess Christ to be truly preached; but manners and
> religion so sincerely reformed, I have not yet seen in any
> other place.[26]

In the worship of the English Church in Geneva, 'The
Forme of Prayers' was used as a guide. This was the order
compiled by Whittingham and Knox at Frankfurt, but not
printed until Knox and his supporters settled in Geneva.
With only minor alterations it was to become the Book of
Common Order of the Church of Scotland (Extract XXIV, p
101 and Extract XXV, p 105).

About the time of his second son Eleazar's birth in
November 1558, Knox received another invitation to return
to Scotland. Understandably he was not anxious to leave his
wife and sons at such a time. Indeed on 16 December 1558
Knox and his friend Christopher Goodman were elected

pastors of the English congregation in Geneva for the coming year. But on 28 January 1559 Knox left Geneva, having arranged for Goodman to look after his wife and family and Mrs Bowes.

Two events, one in Scotland and one in England, had made him change his mind about returning to Scotland. A Common Band or Covenant had been drawn up and signed by John Erskine of Dun, the Earls of Argyll, Glencairn and Morton and the Lord of Lorne. This pledged the signatories to defend the Evangel of Christ and his congregation from the rage of Satan and Antichrist with their whole power, substance and very lives. They promised to maintain faithful ministers who would purely and truly preach Christ's Evangel and give his Sacraments to his people. They also publicly renounced the existing Church structure and 'all the superstitions, abomination and idolatry thereof.'[27] This meant that there was now in Scotland an organised group of influential laymen committed to Reform.

On 17 November 1558 Mary Tudor, Queen of England, died and was succeeded by her half-sister, Elizabeth. This transformed the situation in England—she was a Protestant, by necessity if not conviction, since the Pope regarded her as illegitimate. But it also changed things in Geneva—in January 1559 most of Knox's congregation returned to England.

Knox reached Dieppe on 19 February, hoping to get a passport to travel through England. But he had offended Queen Elizabeth with his remarks about the rule of women and no passport was forthcoming. His enforced extended stay in Dieppe was by no means inactive, for he acted as pastor of the Reformed congregation there and learned a good deal about the organisation of the French Reformed Synod. Eventually he decided that he would have to sail the whole way to Scotland and he arrived at Leith on 2 May 1559.

THE CRISIS 1559-60

MARY of Guise, the Queen Mother, had succeeded the Earl
of Arran as Regent in 1554, but until 1559 had done little
to impede the progress of Reform in the Church. She had
even deplored the cruelty of Archbishop John Hamilton
in having an aged priest called Walter Myln burnt for heresy
in April 1558. But in 1559 she decided to confront the
growing Reform movement. Her daughter, Mary, Queen of
Scots, had married Francis, the Dauphin of France, and she
had secured for Francis the title of King of Scots. Feeling
that she could now count on French military help, she was
prepared to take action against the Reforming preachers and
the nobles and gentlemen who supported them. In March
1559 the Regent forbade anyone to celebrate the Communion except priests acting under ecclesiastical authority.
At Easter, Paul Methven gave communion to large congregations in Dundee and John Willock did the same at Ayr.
The Regent replied by summoning Methven, Willock and
two other preachers to appear before the Privy Council at
Stirling on 10 May to answer charges of usurping the authority of the Church and preaching heresy and sedition.

When Knox arrived in Edinburgh the bishops were all
assembled for a provincial synod, but they were unwilling to
act against him without the authority of the Regent who
was in Glasgow. By the time the bishops had communicated
with the Regent, Knox had departed for Dundee. A notable
succession of sermons began with a sermon in St John's Kirk in
Perth which Knox describes as 'vehement against idolatry'

When a priest soon afterwards began to celebrate mass, a riot was provoked and much damage was done in the Kirk and also in the Charterhouse and the houses of the Black and Grey Friars. On 11 June, Knox fulfilled his own prophecy and preached once more in the Parish Church of St Andrews where he had received his call to be a preacher. On 29 June he preached in St Giles in Edinburgh. All this was possible because the army raised by the Protestant Lords had twice faced up to the Regent's army and had compelled it to withdraw. Furthermore, Lord James Stewart, an illegitimate son of James V and titular Prior of St Andrews, had joined the Reforming party.

The success was more apparent than real and both sides appealed for help: the Regent from France and the Reformers from England. The accession of the Dauphin Francis to the French throne in 1559 seemed to make effective help from France more likely. The English Queen was slow to commit herself to helping rebels against another woman ruler. The Regent was able to occupy Leith and began to strengthen its fortifications to provide a secure landing place for the expected reinforcements from France. The Reforming party made rather ineffective efforts to besiege Leith and then gave up and retired to Stirling.

Knox had been preaching in Edinburgh on the eightieth Psalm but his sermon on verses 4-6 was preached in Stirling before the leaders of the Reforming party, including the Duke of Chatelherault who had changed sides and joined them. He had been replaced, when Earl of Arran, as Regent by the Queen Mother and had been given the French dukedom by the way of compensation. In his application of the Psalmist's words, 'Thou hast made us a strife unto our neighbours and our enemies laugh us to scorn amongst themselves', Knox does not mince his words:

When we were a few number, in comparison of our
enemies, when we had neither Earl nor Lord (a few
excepted) to comfort us, we called upon God; we took
him for our protector, defence, and only refuge. Amongst
us was heard no bragging of multitude, of our strength,
nor policy; we did only sob to God to have respect to the
equity of our cause, and to the cruel pursuit of the tyrant-
ful enemy. But since that our number hath been thus
multiplied, and chiefly since my Lord Duke's Grace with
his friends have been joined with us, there was nothing
heard but 'This Lord will bring these many hundred
spears; this man hath the credit to persuade this country;
if this Earl be ours, no man in such a bounds will trouble
us.'

Knox has no hesitation in reminding the Duke and his friends
that until recently they were on the other side:

I am assured that neither he, neither yet his friends, did
feel before this time the anguish and grief of hearts which
we felt when, in their blind fury, they pursued us.

But Knox does not see the situation as hopeless. They must
all turn to the Eternal our God and if they do so unfeignedly:

I no more doubt but that this our dolour, confusion, and
fear shall be turned into joy, honour, and boldness than
that I doubt that God gave victory to the Israelites over
the Benjamites, after that twice with ignominy they were
repulsed and driven back. Yea, whatsoever shall become
of us and of our mortal carcasses, I doubt not but that
this cause (in despite of Satan) shall prevail in the realm
of Scotland.[28]

This sermon probably marks the end of Knox's political effectiveness. He retired to St Andrews where his wife and sons were now in residence. Although he was largely an observer of the events of the following eight months, Knox secured during his time at St Andrews the decisive support of John Douglas, the Rector of the University, and the conversion of John Winram, sub-prior of St Andrews.

Knox may well have doubted the value of Chatelherault to the Reformed cause, but the Duke's adherence enabled Queen Elizabeth to agree to the Treaty of Berwick between herself and 'the noble and mighty Prince, James, Duke of Chatelherault, second person of the realm of Scotland'. With effective English help, the siege of Leith was resumed.

The crisis was resolved by the sudden death of Mary of Guise on 11 June 1560. A treaty was signed between England and France by which the French agreed to withdraw all their troops from Scotland. The Scots were not parties to the treaty, but in an appendix Mary and Francis were represented as making 'concessions' to their Scottish subjects. The most important of these was the provision that the Estates of Parliament should meet on 1 August 1560.

Knox was not a member of the Parliament but in April 1560 he had been settled as one of the ministers of Edinburgh and he preached from the prophecy of Haggai during its sitting. His application of his text was so pointed that one member remarked, 'We must now forget ourselves and bear the barrow to build the houses of God.'[29] But for all that he preached so vehemently, Knox surely must have been disappointed at the outcome of the Parliament's deliberations. He would certainly have approved of the abolition of the Pope's authority and the prohibition of the Mass, but the Confession of Faith which was accepted by the Parliament was a compromise document which cannot entirely reflect

Knox's views, especially with regard to the position of the civil magistrate.[30] The Book of Discipline, an ambitious plan for a Christian commonwealth, which had been drafted as early as May 1560, was not submitted and was approved in a revised form only by the Great Council in January 1561. It was never to have any statutory force.

The last weeks of 1560 saw two deaths which are recorded by Knox in his *History of the Reformation in Scotland*. He is characteristically reticent about the first, remarking only that he was 'in no small heaviness by reason of the late death of his dear bedfellow, Marjory Bowes.'[31] He is somewhat waspish about the death of Francis II, the husband of Mary, Queen of Scots: 'For as the said King sat at Mass, he was suddenly stricken with an apposthume in that deaf ear that never would hear the truth of God.'[32]

MINISTER AT EDINBURGH

ONE of the provisions of the Book of Discipline which was implemented was the election of Superintendents. The office was to be no sinecure:

> These men must not be suffered to live as your idle Bishops have done heretofore; neither must they remain where gladly they would. But they must be preachers themselves, and such as may make no long residence in any one place, till their churches be planted and provided of Ministers, or at the least of Readers.[33]

Not surprisingly his colleagues were keen that Knox should accept office as a Superintendent. He had fulfilled a not dissimilar role in England while a chaplain to Edward VI. But he refused, perhaps on grounds of his health which had begun to deteriorate, although he was only 46. John Spottiswoode was appointed as Superintendent of Lothian and was formally admitted to office at a service in Edinburgh at which Knox gave the Exhortation (Extract XXVI, p 108)

According to Thomas Randolph, the English Queen's agent in Scotland, Knox was well pleased with his position as Minister at Edinburgh:

> Mr Knox thinketh his state honourable enough, if God give him strength to persist in that vocation that he hath placed him in, and will receive no other.[34]

The burgh council seemed anxious to make Knox as comfortable as possible. When he took up residence in a house in Trunk Close on the north side of the High Street, the council paid the rent to the landlord and also paid for the furnishings of the house and for a lock for the door. Later on, the Dean of the Crafts was ordered to build a warm study for Knox. He stayed in this house until Michaelmas 1565 when he moved to another house.

Knox had scarcely settled in his house at Trunk Close when his wife Marjory died at the early age of 24, leaving Knox with two young sons, Nathaniel aged three and a half and Eleazer only two. Mrs Bowes went to England after her daughter's death, but in August 1562 Randolph arranged for permission to let her leave England and return to Edinburgh:

> My other request proceedeth from Mr Knox, who now, as he sayeth, is a sole man, by reason of the absence of his mother-in-law, Mistress Bowes, who is willing to return again into this country, if she had the Queen's Majesty's licence for herself, her man, and one maid, with a passport for her three horses, of the which two shall return; and to take with her so much money as she hath of her own, the sum not exceeding one hundred pounds sterling. This is his humble suit unto your Honour, and that he trusteth shall not be denied unto him, assuring your honour that only this is meant herein, that she may be a relief unto him in the burden of household and bringing up of his children, her daughter's sons.[35]

Mrs Bowes remained with Knox until his marriage to Margaret Stewart in the autumn of 1564; after which Mrs Bowes returned to England.

A great matter of concern for Knox during his ministry
at Edinburgh was the Queen's insistence on having Mass
said in her private chapel at Holyrood. Mary, Queen of Scots,
widowed by the death of Francis II of France, had decided
to return to her own realm. On the Sunday after her arrival
in August 1561, Mass was said at Holyrood, the door to
the chapel being guarded by none other than Lord James
Stewart. Knox was not impressed with his excuse that he
was preventing 'all Scottish men to enter in to the Mass',[36]
and the following Sunday he declared:

> That one Mass [there was no more suffered at the first]
> was more fearful to him than if ten thousand armed
> enemies were landed in any part of the realm, of purpose
> to suppress the whole religion. For [said he] in our God
> there is strength to resist and confound multitudes if
> we unfeignedly depend upon him; whereof heretofore
> we have had experience; but when we join hands with
> idolatry, it is no doubt but that both God's amicable
> presence and comfortable defence leaveth us, and what
> shall then become of us?[37]

Shortly after preaching this sermon, Knox had a stormy
interview with the Queen who accused him of fomenting
trouble in past years in England and now in Scotland. Knox
defended his record in England:

> For in England I was resident only the space of five years.
> The places were Berwick, where I abode two years; so
> long in the New Castle; and a year in London. Now,
> Madam, if in any of these places, during the time that I
> was there, any man shall be able to prove that there was
> either battle, sedition or mutiny I shall confess that I

myself was the malefactor and the shedder of the blood.
I ashame not, Madam, further to affirm that God so
blessed my weak labours that in Berwick (where commonly before there used to be slaughter by reason of
quarrels that used to arise amongst soldiers) there was
as great quietness all the time that I remained there as
there is this day in Edinburgh.[38]

When the Queen accused Knox of preventing her subjects
from giving her due obedience, he replied, 'God forbid that
ever I take upon me to command any to obey me, or yet to
set subjects at liberty to do what pleaseth them. But my
travail is that both princes and subjects obey God'.[39]

This was the first of several interviews with the Queen,
in all of which there was little or no meeting of minds.
When the Queen demanded, 'What have ye to do with my
marriage? Or what are ye within this Commonwealth?'
Knox replied, 'A subject born within the same, Madam.
And albeit I neither be Earl, Lord, nor Baron within it, yet
has God made me (how object that ever I be in your eyes) a
profitable member within the same.' The Queen burst into
tears of rage, at which Knox made a reference to his problem
as a father, 'Madam, in God's presence I speak. I never
delighted in the weeping of any of God's creatures; yea I can
scarcely well abide the tears of my own boys whom my own
hand corrects, much less can I rejoice in your Majesty's
weeping.'[40]

In the summer of 1564 the Earl of Lennox and his son,
Lord Darnley, came to Scotland. The Queen fell in love with
Darnley, a handsome youth of 18 years. In July 1565 they
were married and Mary conferred on her new husband the
title of King. In great state King Henry came to hear Knox
preach in St Giles on 19 August 1565. Because the sermon

gave great offence to the Court, and because Knox was forbidden to preach while the King and Queen were in Edinburgh, he set to work to put it down on paper for publication, thus giving us the only complete sermon we have from his pen (Extract XXVII, p 110). In his preface he says wryly:

> If any man think it easy unto me to mitigate by my pen the inconsiderate sharpness of my tongue, and so can not men freely judge of that my Sermon, I answer, that neither am I so impudent that I will study to abuse the world in this great light, neither yet so void of fear of my God, that I will avow a lie in His own presence.[41]

Knox also explains that he considers himself to be a preacher rather than a writer (Extract XXVIII, p 113).

Despite this claim, the most important achievement of this period was probably Knox's *History of the Reformation in Scotland* which he had begun to write in 1559 and for which he continued to gather materials as late as 1571. He did not live to finish it and none of it was published until after his death. It is a remarkable testimony from one of the leading participants in the Reformation movement rather than an objective history, but it is a valuable source of information which all subsequent historians of the period can ignore only at their peril.

Knox was not at his happiest when engaging in debate with supporters of the old ways of worship—like Quintin Kennedy, Abbot of Crossraguel and Ninian Winzet, the deprived master of the school at Linlithgow. Knox could not understand Kennedy's argument that when the high priest Melchizedek provided bread and wine for Abraham and his retainers, he was prefiguring the Mass. He failed to answer

Winzet's claim that Knox was not a lawful minister because he performed no miracles. By the time that he writes up his account of another debate, this time with the Jesuit, James Tyrie, Knox can only say: 'As the world is weary of me, so am I of it.'[42] It is good to have the moving prayer which is attached to this account (see Extract XXXII, p 120).

THE LAST YEARS

BECAUSE of the civil war that broke out after the deposition of Mary, Queen of Scots, John Knox was forced to leave Edinburgh and he went to stay in St Andrews in July 1571, lodging in the old priory near St Leonard's College. A young student in that College, James Melville, pays this tribute to the Reformer: 'In all my course the greatest benefit was the sight and hearing of that extraordinary man of God, Mr John Knox'.[43]

Knox was obviously far from well, but he embarked on a course of sermons on the Book of Daniel. Melville went along to hear him and to take notes:

I had my pen and my little book, and took away such things as I could comprehend. In the opening up of his text he was moderate the space of an half hour; but when he entered to application, he made me so to grew [*ie* shudder] and tremble, that I could not hold a pen to write.[44]

On another occasion, Melville recalls, Knox was so weak that he had to be helped into the pulpit, but before he was done with his sermon 'he was so active and vigorous that he was like to ding that pulpit in blads, and fly out of it!'[45]

A truce in the civil war enabled Knox to return to Edinburgh in August 1572, but when he preached in St Giles on the last day of the month his voice was so weak that many of the congregation could not hear him. It was impossible for

him to stop preaching, so he arranged for services to be held
in the Tolbooth and officiated there for two months. On
Sunday 9 November he preached as usual in the Tolbooth
and then went to St Giles to take part in the induction of his
successor, James Lawson. He never went out again.

In his last days Knox was cared for by his secretary,
Richard Bannatyne and by his wife, Margaret Stewart. On
Monday 24 November 1572 he took a turn for the worse
and asked his wife about noon to read to him the 15th
chapter of I Corinthians. Five hours later he asked her, 'Go
read where I cast my first anchor' and she read the 17th
chapter of the Gospel according to John. After evening
prayers, about eleven o' clock, he died.[46]

At the funeral two days later, the Earl of Morton, who
had just been appointed Regent, said of Knox:

Here lyeth a man, who in his life never feared the face of
man; who hath been often threatened with dagge and
dagger, but yet hath ended his days in peace and honour.[47]

Notes to Part 1

1   *Calderwood* I, 155 f.
2   *Laing* VI, p 643.
3   *Laing* VI, p 104.
4   *Lorimer*, pp 290-2.
5   *Laing* III, p 34.
6   *Laing* III, p 34, 52.
7   *Laing* III, p 368.
8   *Laing* III, p 106.
9   *Laing* III, p 107.
10 *Laing* III, p 133.
11 *Laing* III, p 122.
12 *Laing* III, p 120.
13 *Laing* III, p 225.
14 *Laing* III, p 236.
15 *Laing* III, p 296.
16 *Laing* IV, p 217.
17 *Laing* IV, p 218.
18 *Laing* VI, p 516.
19 *Laing* IV, p 218.
20 *Dickinson* I, p 120.
21 *Laing* IV, p 78.
22 *Laing* IV, p 79.
23 *Dickinson* I, p 123.
24 *Laing* IV, p 251.
25 ibid.
26 *Laing* IV, p 240.
27 *Dickinson* I, pp 136 f.

28 *Dickinson* I, p 269 f.
29 *Dickinson* I, p 335 (*Calderwood* II, p 12). The comment is attributed by Calderwood to William Maitland of Lethington.
30 *Laing* VI, pp 120 ff.
31 *Dickinson* I, p 351.
32 *Dickinson* I, pp 348 f.
33 *Dickinson* II, p 292.
34 Laing VI, p 122.
35 *Laing* VI, p 141.
36 *Dickinson* II, p 8.
37 *Dickinson* II, p 12.
38 *Dickinson* II, p 15.
39 *Dickinson* II, p 17.
40 *Dickinson* II, p 83.
41 *Laing* VI, p 230.
42 *Laing* VI, p 514.
43 *Melville*, p 31.
44 *Melville*, p 26.
45 *Melville*, p 33.
46 *Laing* VI, pp 642-4.
47 *Laing* VI, p lii.

BIBLIOGRAPHY AND KEY
TO WORKS CITED IN PART 1

Calderwood, David, *The History of the Kirk of Scotland* (Edinburgh 1842) (*Calderwood*).

Dickinson, William Croft (ed), *John Knox's History of the Reformation in Scotland* (Edinburgh 1949) (*Dickinson*).

Laing, David (ed), *The Works of John Knox* (Edinburgh 1895) (*Laing*).

Lorimer, Peter, *John Knox and the Church of England* (London 1875) (*Lorimer*).

Melville, James, *Autobiography and Diary* (Edinburgh 1842) (*Melville*).

* * *

Breslow, Marvin A (ed), *The Political Writings of John Knox: First Blast of the Trumpet Against the Monstrous Regement of Women, and Other Selected Works* (Folger Books, USA 1985).

Thomson, Thomas (ed), *Select Practical Writings of John Knox* (Edinburgh 1845).

* * *

Bowen, Marjorie, *The Life of John Knox* (London 1940, 1949).

Brown, P Hume, *John Knox, A Biography* (London 1895).

Donaldson, Gordon, *John Knox* (London 1983).

Innes, A Taylor, *John Knox* (Edinburgh 1896).

Lamont, Stewart, *The Swordbearer, John Knox and the European Reformation* (London 1991).

Lang, Andrew, *John Knox and the Reformation* (London 1905).

McCrie, Thomas, *Life of John Knox* (Edinburgh 1831).

Muir, Edwin, *John Knox: portrait of a Calvinist* (London 1929).

Percy, Lord Eustace, *John Knox* (London 1937, 1964).

Reid, W Stanford, *Trumpeter of God, A Biography of John Knox* (New York 1974).

Ridley, Jasper, *John Knox* (Oxford 1968).

Shaw, Duncan (ed), *John Knox, A Quatercentenary Reappraisal* (Edinburgh, Saint Andrew Press 1975).

Whitley, Elizabeth, *Plain Mr Knox* (London 1960).

* * *

Greaves, Richard L, *Theology and Revolution in the Scottish Reformation, Studies in the Thought of John Knox* (Grand Rapids, Michigan 1980).

Kyle, Richard G, *The Mind of John Knox* (Lawrence, Kansas 1984).

McEwen, James S, *The Faith of John Knox* (London 1961, 1962).

JOHN KNOX
Part 2: Extracts from Knox's Writings

INTRODUCTION

THE extracts in Part 2 are chosen to illustrate the devotional facets of Knox's thought and so the more controversial and political writings are only slightly represented. As it is virtually impossible to identify Knox's contributions to the Confession of Faith and the Book of Discipline, no extracts are given from either. Both were compromise and 'committee' documents.

Apart from the first, the extracts are arranged chronologically in order to show the development of Knox's spirituality. Most are referred to in Part 1. They are taken mainly from the 1895 edition of David Laing's collection of Knox's Works. Punctuation and capitalisation follow Laing, but the spelling has been modernised and some long paragraphs divided. For the *History of the Reformation in Scotland,* Professor Croft Dickinson's 1949 edition has been used. Two documents not included in Laing have been taken from Peter Lorimer's *John Knox and the Church of England* and in the extracts from them the spelling has also been modernised. In order to give the flavour of the original, the titles in the Bibliography to Part 2 have been given in their original spelling. References have been given so that the reader who is interested may go further.

Those who find the old, erratic spelling a hindrance should seek out Thomas Thomson's *Select Practical Writings of John Knox* which was to some extent the model for this book, but which includes complete works with modern spelling.

I

THE HIGH PRIESTLY PRAYER
OF CHRIST

[This extract from his lengthy treatise on Predestination may contain a clue about Knox's conversion.]

PLAIN it is, that the counsel of God is stable, and his love immutable towards his Elect, because (all other conditions set apart) Christ affirmeth, That the life everlasting pertaineth to them that are given by God, and received by him in protection and safeguard. But more plainly doth he speak in that his solemn prayer; for after that by divers means he had comforted the sorrowful hearts of his Disciples, he giveth comfort to the whole Church, affirming, 'That he did not pray only for those that there were present with him, but also for all those that should after believe, by their preaching, in him.' These words he added for our singular comfort: 'I have given unto them the glory which thou hast given to me; that they may be one, as we are one; I in them, and thou in me, that they may be made perfect in one; and that the world may know, that thou hast sent me, and that thou hast loved them as thou hast loved me.' O that our hearts could, without contradiction, embrace these words; for then with humility should we prostrate ourselves before our God, and with unfeigned tears give thanks for his mercy!

Three things in these words are to be observed; First that the same glory which God the Father hath given to his Son, the same hath he given to such as believe in him. Not that either Christ Jesus had then the full glory, as he was man, for as yet he had not overcome the death; neither that his Elect at any time in this life can attain to the fruition of the same, but that the one was as assured in God's immutable counsel as was the other. For as the Head should overcome the bitter death, and so triumph over Satan the author thereof, so should his members in the time appointed; as he doth further express, saying, 'I will, Father, that where that I am, there also be those which thou hast given unto me, that they may see my glory.'

The second is, that so straight and near is the conjunction and union betwixt Christ Jesus and his members, that they must be one, and never can be separated. For so did Christ pray, saying, 'That they all may be one, as we are one: I in them and thou in me, that they may be made perfect in one.' Let the conjunction be diligently marked, for much it serveth to our comfort. As the Godhead is inseparably joined with the humanity in Christ Jesus our Lord, so the one, that is the Godhead, neither could nor can leave the humanity at any time, how bitter that ever the storms appeared; so can not Christ Jesus leave his dear spouse the Church, neither yet any true member of the same. For that he includeth under the general word 'all' for any accident, how horrible that ever it be, that came to pass in their life. And albeit that this appear strange, and also a doctrine that may seem to give liberty to sin, yet may not the children of God be defrauded of their food, because that dogs will abuse the same. But of this we shall (God willing) after speak.

The third thing to be noted is, That the love of God towardes his Elect, given to Christe, is immutable. For Christ putteth it in equal balance with the love by which his Father loved him. Not that I would any man should so understand me, as that I placed any man in equal dignity and glory with Christ Jesus touching his office. No, that must be reserved

wholly and only to himself; that he is the only Beloved, in
whom all the rest are beloved; that he is the Head, that only
giveth life to the body; and that he is the sovereign Prince,
before whom all knee shall bow. But I mean, that as the love
of God the Father was ever constant towards his dear Son, so
is it also towardes the members of his body; yea even when
they are ignorant and enemies unto him, as the Apostle witnesseth, saying, 'God specially commendeth his love towards
us, that when we were yet sinners Christ died for us; much
more being justified now by his blood, we shall be saved by
him from wrath. For if, when we were enemies, we were
reconciled to God by the death of his Son, much more, we,
being reconciled, shall be saved by his life.'

Laing V, pp 51-52
{spelling modernised}

II

KNOX'S CALL
TO BE A PREACHER

[Speaking of himself in the third person Knox includes this account of his Call in his 'History of the Reformation in Scotland'.]

BECAUSE he had the care of some gentlemen's children, whom certain years he had nourished in godliness, their fathers solicited him [*ie* Knox] to go to Saint Andrews, that himself might have the benefit of the Castle, and their children the benefit of his doctrine; and so (we say) came he the time foresaid to the said place, and, having in his company Francis Douglas of Longniddry, George his brother, and Alexander Cockburn, eldest son then to the Laird of Ormiston, began to exercise them after his accustomed manner. Besides their grammar, and other humane authors, he read unto them a catechism, an account whereof he caused them give publicly in the Parish Kirk of Saint Andrews. He read moreover unto them the Evangel of John, proceeding where he left at his departing from Longniddry, where before his residence was; and that lecture he read in the chapel, within the Castle, at a certain hour. They of the place, but especially Master Henry Balnaves and John Rough, preacher, perceiving the manner of his doctrine, began earnestly to travail with him, that he would take the preaching place upon him. But he utterly refused, alleging, 'That he would not run where God had not called him'; meaning that he would do nothing without a lawful vocation.

Whereupon they privily amongst themselves advising,

45

having with them in council Sir David Lindsay of the
Mount, they concluded, that they would give a charge to the
said John, and that publicly, by the mouth of their preacher.
And so upon a certain day, a sermon was had of the election
of ministers: What power the congregation (how small that
ever it was, passing the number of two or three) had above
any man, in whom they supposed and espied the gifts of
God to be, and how dangerous it was to refuse, and not to
hear the voice of such as desire to be instructed. These and
other heads (we say), declared, the said John Rough, preacher,
directed his words to the said John Knox, saying, 'Brother,
ye shall not be offended, albeit that I speak unto you that
which I have in charge, even from all those that are here
present, which is this: In the name of God, and of his Son
Jesus Christ, and in the name of these that presently calls
you by my mouth, I charge you, that ye refuse not this holy
vocation, but that as ye tender the glory of God, the increase
of Christ his kingdom, the edification of your brethren, and
the comfort of me, whom ye understand well enough to be
oppressed by the multitude of labours, that ye take upon you
the public office and charge of preaching, even as ye look
to avoid God's heavy displeasure, and desire that he shall
multiply his graces with you.' And in the end he said to
those that were present, 'Was not this your charge to me?
And do ye not approve this vocation?' They answered, 'It
was; and we approve it.' Whereat the said John, abashed,
burst forth in most abundant tears, and withdrew himself to
his chamber. His countenance and behaviour, from that day
till the day that he was compelled to present himself to the
public place of preaching, did sufficiently declare the grief
and trouble of his heart; for no man saw any sign of mirth of
him neither yet had he pleasure to accompany any man,
many days together.   *Dickinson I, pp 82 f*

III

KNOX'S FIRST SERMON

[Knox gives the following summary of his first sermon, preached in the Parish Church of St Andrews in 1547.]

AND so the next Sunday was appointed to the said John to express his mind in the public preaching place. Which day approaching, the said John took the text written in Daniel, the seventh chapter, beginning thus: 'And another king shall rise after them and he shall be unlike unto the first, and he shall subdue three kings, and shall speak words against the Most High, and shall consume the saints of the Most High, and think that he may change times and laws, and they shall be given into his hands, until a time, and times, and dividing of times.'

1. In the beginning of his sermon, he showed the great love of God towards his Church, whom it pleaseth to forewarn of dangers to come so many years before they come to pass. 2. He briefly entreated the estate of the Israelites, who then were in bondage in Babylon, for the most part; and made a short discourse of the four Empires, the Babylonian, the Persian, that of the Greeks, and the fourth of the Romans; in the destruction whereof, rose up that last Beast, which he affirmed to be the Roman Church: for to none other power that ever has yet been, do all the notes of the Beast that God has shown to the Prophet appertain, except to it alone; and unto it they do so properly appertain, that such as are not more than blind, may clearly see them. 3. But before he began

to open the corruptions of the Papistry, he defined the true
Kirk, showed the true notes of it, whereupon it was built,
why it was the pillar of verity, and why it could not err, to
wit, 'Because it heard the voice of its own pastor, Jesus Christ,
would not hear a stranger, neither yet would be carried
about with every kind of doctrine'.

Dickinson I, pp 84 f

IV

JUSTIFICATION

[In the winter of 1548 Henry Balnaves, a prisoner in the old palace of Rouen, sent to John Knox, a prisoner in a French galley, a treatise on Justification. Knox prepared a summary of the treatise as he felt that it expressed his own views. The following paragraphs are taken from that summary.]

OUR whole study should be to adhere unto God; running to him in the time of tribulation, (as doth the wild hart in the burning heat to the cold river), with sure hope of deliverance by him alone; not inquiring his name, that is, the manner how he shall deliver us.

By Faith have we knowledge of God, whom we should seek in his Scriptures, and receive him as he is offered to us thereinto; that is, a Defender, Protector, Refuge and Father inquiring no further speculation of him. For, Philip desiring to see the Father, answered Christ, 'Who hath seen me hath seen the Father.' Meaning that the love, goodness and mercy, which God the Father beareth unto mankind, he had expressed in doctrine and works; and also should show a most singular token of love, giving his own life for his enemies. And therefore would all men come to him, to whom the Father hath given all power.

* * *

By bodily afflictions our faith is tried, as gold by the fire.

49

They are also a communion with the passions of Jesus Christ. And therefore in them have we matter and cause to rejoice, considering we suffer without cause, committed contrary man. Notwithstanding, the wicked persecute the faithful in all ages as if they had been mischievous or evil doers; as may be seen in the persecution of the Prophets, Apostles, and of Jesus Christ himself. The cause hereof is the neglecting of God's Word, and taking from Faith her due office, whereof riseth all dishonouring of God; for none may or can honour God except the justified man.

And albeit, in diverse men there be diverse opinions of Justification; yet they alone, in whom the Holy Spirit worketh true Faith (which never wanteth good works) are just before God. The substance of Justification is, to cleave fast unto God, by Jesus Christ, and not by our self, nor yet by our works. And this article of Justification should be holden in recent memory, because without the knowledge thereof, no works are pleasant before God.

* * *

Seeing then our Forefathers were not just by the Law, nor works thereof, of necessity must we seek the Justice of another (that is of Jesus Christ) which the Law may not accuse. In whom if we believe, we are received in the favour of God, accepted as just without our merits or deservings.

* * *

The Justice which is acceptable before God hath diverse names. First, it is called the Justice of God, because it proceedeth onely of the mercy of God. Secondly, it is called the Justice of Faith, because Faith is the instrument whereby we apprehend the mercy of God. And last, it is called Justice because by Faith in Christ, it is given us freely without our deservings. But even as the dry land receiveth the rain but all deservings of the self; so receive we the justice, which is of value before God, without all our works: but yet we must suffer God to work in us. And this Justice is plainly revealed in the Evangel, from faith to faith, that is, we should continue in this faith all our life. For the just live by faith, ever trusting to obtain that which is promised, which is eternal life, promised to us by Jesus Christ.

Laing II, pp 13-20
{spelling modernised}

V

THE DUTIES OF CHRISTIANS
ACCORDING TO VOCATION

[These paragraphs are also taken from Knox's Summary of the Henry Balnaves treatise on Justification.]

ALL Estate of man is contained within one of these four special vocations: either he is Prince or subject, Pastor or one of the flock, Father or son, Lord or servant.

* * *

In the Prince is contained all magistrates having jurisdiction in a commonweal; whose duty is, First, to know God, and his law, which hath placed them in that authority. Secondly, To guide, feed and defend their subjects; knowing themselves to be no better of their nature than is the poorest in their realm. Thirdly, To defend the just, and punish the wicked, but respect of persons, having their hearts and eyes clean and pure from all avarice. They are called the sons of God, and should be obeyed in all things not repugning to the command of God; because they are ordained and placed by God to punish vice and maintain virtue: And therefore their own life should be pure and clean; first because otherwise they can not punish sin; and secondly, because the wickedness of princes provoketh their subjects to the imitation thereof; and therefore the life of princes should be pure and clean, as a mirror to their subjects; and should admit into their kingdoms no worshipping of God, except that which is commanded in the Scriptures. For God, being commoved by idolatry and strange worshipping, hath destroyed many kingdoms, as all prophesyings witness.

The principal office of a Bishop is to preach the true Evangel of Jesus Christ; knowing that if the flock perish, the blood shall be required at his hands; and that he, neglecting the preaching of the Evangel, is no bishop nor can do no work pleasing before God. And therefore no bishop should mix himself with temporal or secular business, for that is contrary his vocation; but continually should preach, read and exhort his flock to seek their spiritual food in the Scriptures.

* * *

The office of the Father (under whom is comprehended all householders) is to rule and guide his children, family and servants, in all godliness and honesty, instructing them in the law and Word of God.... The office of the Husband is, to love and defend his wife, giving to her only his body. The office of the Wife is likewise, to love and obey her husband, usurping no dominion over him. And the office of them both is, to instruct their children in God's law; giving ever to them example of good life, and holding them at godly occupations; labouring also themselves faithfully for sustentation of their families.

The office and duty of the Lord is, to pay his servants the reward promised. And the office of the Servant is, to work faithfully and labour, to the profit and utility of his lord, but fraud or simulation, as he would serve Jesus Christ. The office of the Subject is, to obey his prince and rulers placed by him; giving unto them honour, custom, and tribute, not requiring the cause why they receive the same; for that pertaineth not to the vocation of a subject. The office of the Son is to love, fear, and honour his parents; which honour standeth not in words only, but in ministring of all things necessary unto them; which if the Son do not to the father and mother, he can do no good work before God.

Laing III, pp 25-27
{spelling modernised}

VI

A Summary, according to the Holy Scriptures, of the Sacrament of The Lord's Supper 1550

[*This short statement is annexed to Knox's 'Vindication of the Doctrine that the Mass is idolatry'.*]

HERE is briefly declared in a sum, according to the Holy Scriptures, what opinion we Christians have of the Lord's Supper, called The Sacrament of the Body and Blood of our Saviour Jesus Christ.

First, We confess that it is a holy action, ordained of God, in the which the Lord Jesus, by earthly and visible things set before us, lifteth us up unto heavenly and invisible things. And that when he had prepared his spiritual banquet, he witnessed that he himself was the lively bread wherewith our souls be fed unto everlasting life.

And therefore, in setting furth bread and wine to eat and drink, he confirmeth and sealeth up to us his promise and communion, (that is, that we shall be partakers with him in his kingdom); and representeth unto us, and maketh plain to our senses, his heavenly gifts; and also giveth unto us him self, to be received with faith, and not with mouth, not yet by transfusion of substance. But so through the virtue of Holy Ghost, that we, being fed with his flesh, and refreshed with his blood, may be renewed both unto true godliness and to immortality.

And also that herewith the Lord Jesus gathereth us unto a visible body, so that we be members one of another, and make altogether one body, whereof Jesus Christ is only head.

And finally that by the same Sacrament, the Lord calleth us
to remembrance of his Death and Passion, to stir up our hearts
to praise his most holy name.

Farther more, we acknowledge that this Sacrament ought
to be come unto reverently, considering there is exhibited
and given a testimony of the wonderful society and knitting
together of the Lord Jesus and of the receivers; and also, that
there is included and contained in this Sacrament, that he
will preserve his Kirk. For herein we be commanded to show
the Lord's death until he come.

Also, we believe that it is a Confession, wherein we show
what kind of doctrine we profess; and what Congregation we
join ourselves unto; and likewise, that it is a band of mutual
love amongst us. And finally, we believe that all the comers
unto this holy Supper must bring with them their conversion
unto the Lord, by unfeigned repentance in Faith; and in this
Sacrament receive the seals and confirmation of their faith;
and yet must in no wise think, that for this work's sake their
sins be forgiven.

And as concerning these word, *Hoc est corpus meum*, 'This
is my body', on which the Papists depend so much, saying,
That we must needs believe that the bread and the wine be
transubstantiated into Christ's body and blood; We acknowledge that it is no article of our faith which can save us, nor
which we are bound to believe upon pain of eternal damnation. For if we should believe that his very natural body,
both flesh and blood, were naturally in the bread and wine,
that should not save us, seeing many believe that, and yet
receive it to their damnation. For it is not his presence in
the bread that can save us, but his presence in our hearts
through faith in his blood, which hath washed out our sins,
and pacified his Father's wrath towards us. And again, if we
do not believe his bodily presence in the bread and wine,

that shall not damn us, but the absence out of our heart through unbelief.

Now if they would here object, that though it be truth, that the absence out of the bread could not damn us, yet are we bound to believe it because of God's Word, saying, 'This is my body,' which who believeth not as much as in him lieth, maketh God a liar: and therefore, of an obstinate mind not to believe his Word, may be our damnation. To this we answer, That we believe God's Word, and confess that it is true, but not so to be understood as the Papists grossly affirm. For in the Sacrament we receive Jesus Christ spiritually, as did the Fathers of the Old Testament, according to St Paul's saying. And if men would well weigh, how that Christ, ordaining this Holy Sacrament of his body and blood, spoke these words Sacramentally, doubtless they would never so grossly and foolishly understand them, contrary to all the Scriptures, and to the exposition of St Augustine, St Jerome, Fulgentius, Vigilius, Origen, and many other godly writers.

Laing III, pp 73-5
{spelling modernised}

VII

WHY THE SITTING IN THE ACTION
OF THE LORD'S TABLE
IS PREFERRED TO KNEELING

[*Knox and the other Royal chaplains were asked by the English Privy Council to comment on the 'Forty-two Articles of Religion' which had been drafted by Archbishop Cranmer and others. The following paragraphs are taken from Knox's comments submitted in November 1552.*]

FINALLY, as kneeling is no gesture meet at the Table, so doth it obscure the joyful significations of that holy mystery. Kneeling is the gesture most commonly of suppliants, of beggars, or such men as, greatly troubled by knowledge of misery or offence committed, seeketh help or remission, doubting whether they shall obtain the same or not. But in the Lord's Supper, chiefly in the action of eating and drinking, neither should appear in us dolour, poverty, nor sign of any misery. But commanded to eat and drink by the Lord Jesus in remembrance of him, with glad countenance we ought to obey; and so calling to our mind things that be past, present and to come, all sign and fear of servitude and thralldom ought to be removed; to wit, that we sometimes by nature were the sons of God's wrath, but now by grace recounted and chosen in the number of the sons of God through the faith which is in Jesus our Lord, heirs of God, and fellow heirs with Jesus Christ, in whom we rest, and by whom the Father of Mercy hath caused us to sit amongst heavenly things, and in the whom, at the end, we shall eat and drink at his own table prepared for us in the kingdom of that everlasting Father; of which things the Lord's Table is as it were our assurance and seal, in using whereof all signs of dolour ought to be removed.

But before we take upon us this great honour and dignity we ought to take of ourselves approve and trial; in which we ought not only to lament and bewail our miseries with tears groaning and sobs, asking pardon and mercy for the same, but also ought we to accuse our continuall ingratitude and great unthankfulness, that neither can we abide nor yet at any time be such as it behoveth us to be toward God and our neighbours. Dejected thus in our own sight, and yet erected and raised up through God's free promise, and so commanded by his Son to eat and drink not as beggars (for by grace we are made rich in Christ) but as sons and inheritors whom that victorious King hath placed at his Table—ought we not most gladly to receive the honour and dignity that is offered to us?—seeing that we can not do more honour to God than to obey his voice, and so to prepare ourselves to that holy action that we appear not betrayers of our own faith and hope, which is, that thralldom is taken away, and that we are the children of God, yea, priests and kings, united by Christ's blood; and therefore without doubting or wavering, at Christ's commandment pass we to the Table, not as slaves or servants, but as children of the King and the redeemed people—praising the goodness of him that hath called us to that honour and estate. And therefore taught by Christ's example at his holy Table, we sit as men placed in quietness and in full possession of our Kingdom.

Lorimer, pp 271f
{spelling modernised}

VIII

WHY KNOX GAVE WAY
OVER KNEELING AT
THE LORD'S SUPPER

[The following paragraphs are taken from a letter written by Knox to his congregation in Berwick at the end of the year 1552.]

As touching the chief points of religion I neither will give place (God assisting my infirmity) to man or angel teaching the contrary to that which ye have heard. But as for ceremonies or rites, things of smaller weight, I am not minded to move contention, so that with conscience, and without reproach of my former doctrine, I may avoid the same.

To touch the point, kneeling at the Lord's Supper I have proved by doctrine to be no convenient gesture for a table, which hath been given in that action to such a presence of Christ as no place of God's Scriptures doth teach unto us. And therefore kneeling in that action, appearing to be joined with certain dangers no less in maintaining superstition than in using Christ's holy institution with other gestures than either he used or commanded to be used, I thought good amongst you to avoid, and to use sitting at the Lord's Table, which ye did not refuse, but with all reverence and thanksgiving unto God for his truth, knowing, as I suppose, ye confirmed the doctrine with your gestures and confession. And this day yet, with a testimony of good conscience I signify unto you that I neither repent nor recant that my former doctrine, so do I (for divers causes long to rehearse) much prefer sitting at the Lord's Table either to kneeling standing or going at the action of that mystical supper.

But because I am but one, having in my contrary magistrates, common order, and judgments of many learned, I am not minded for maintenance of that one thing to gainstand the magistrates, in all other and chief points of religion agreeing with Christ and with his true doctrine, nor yet to break nor trouble common order, thought meet to be kept for unity and peace in the congregations for a time. And least of all intend I to dampen or lightly regard the grave judgments of such men as unfeignedly I fear, love and will obey in all things by them judged expedient to promote God's glory—these subsequents granted unto me.

1. First that the magistrates make known (as that they have done if ministers were willing to do their duties) that kneeling is not retained in the Lord's Supper for maintenance of any superstition, much less that any adoration appertaineth to any real presence of Christ's body natural there contained, or joined with those elements of bread and wine, but only for uniform order to be kept, and that for a time, in this Church of England.

2. Secondly that common order claim not kneeling in the Lord's Supper as either necessary or decent to Christ's action, but only as a ceremony thought goodly by man and not by Christ himself; for otherwise shall common order accuse Christ and his action of indecency, or lacking some gesture necessary.

3. And last, that my fathers, whom I fear and honour, and my brethren in labours and profession, whom I unfeignedly love, do not trouble my conscience imputing upon me any foolish enterprise, for that I have, in ministration of Christ's sacraments, more regarded attempting to follow what Christ himself did in his own perfect action than that what any man after hath commanded to be done.

These things granted unto me, I neither will gainstand

godly magistrates, neither break common order nor yet contend with my superiors or fellow preachers, but with patience will I bear that one thing; daily thirsting and calling unto God for reformation of that and others.

Lorimer, p 261f
{spelling modernised}

IX

WHAT IS MEANT
UNDER THE GOSPEL

[This short account of the meaning of the Gospel is included in Knox's letter to his congregation at Berwick in 1552.]

WHAT is meant under the Gospel—First, the infinite goodness of God whose merciful providence hath placed our life and salvation in his only son Jesus Christ, who, of our God, is made to us justice, sanctification, wisdom and redemption.

2. And our Lord Jesus, together with all such gifts as by Him are given to the elect Church of God, as remission of sins, resurrection of the flesh and life everlasting, is the second thing I understand by the Gospel.

3. And the third thing is true faith, which as it only apprehendeth and understandeth all these precedents, so doth it only justify before God, without all respect of works bypast, present or to come; which good works hath God our Father prepared that we his children, adopted and chosen in Christ Jesus, before the foundation of the world was laid, to life everlasting, should walk in them, which is the fourth thing I conclude within the Gospel, to wit:

4. A holy and godly conversation wherein we should obey our God all the days of our life, to the praise and glory of his holy name who hath appointed us to his heirs, when yet we were not.

5. And last, under the Gospel I understand Invocation unto God alone by Jesus Christ, and thanksgiving unto him for his great benefits received; which sometimes are private,

while man alone, in any tribulation, necessity or action, incalls the aid and help of his God for Christ his Son's sake; but are commanded openly to be done, in participation of Christ's Sacraments, left and commanded to be used in his Church for sealing up and better memory to be had of those benefits, that we have received by the communion that we have with Christ Jesus in his body and blood.

Lorimer, p 258
{spelling modernised}

X

A LETTER
OF REASSURANCE

*[The following paragraphs are part of a letter written to Mrs
Elizabeth Bowes by John Knox from Newcastle. He addresses her as
Mother since he is now pledged in marriage to her daughter, Marjory.]*

DEAR Mother, my duty compels me to advertise you, that in
comparing your sins with the sins of Sodom and Gomorrha
ye do not well, but thereunto ye offend, because ye impute
unto God's Holy Spirit a spot wha only has preserved you
from such horrible iniquity; yet ye as an unthankful receiver
does not acknowledge the same, but rather accuses your self
of such abominable crimes, as God forbid that ever ye should
commit. Mother, like as the man offends that excuses his
offence, so he that confessed crime where none is committed,
is injurious to the power and operation of God, for he renders
not unto God due thanks for that whilk he has received.
But, Mother, the cause of this your unthankfulness I take to
be ignorance in you, that ye know not what were the sins of
Sodom and Gomorrha.

* * *

Do you think that every stirring and motion of the flesh, or
yet every ardent and burning lust, is the sin of Sodom? God
forbid that so ye shall think. Does not Paul teach unto you,
that the flesh lusteth against the spirit, even in them of
maist perfection? Doth he not cry and bewail him self in

65

these words: 'O wretched and unhappy man that I am, wha shall deliver me frae this body of death'; and yet the same Apostle, immediately thereafter, as it were rejoicing against sin and death, affirms, 'that there is no condemnation unto such as be in Christ Jesus.' Mark well, the Apostle says not, There is no sin in them that are in Christ Jesus, but there is no condemnation unto them *etc.*

*   *   *

Remember, Mother, that Jesus the Son of God came not in the flesh to call the just (not that any such can be found, but there is that so esteems themselves), but he came to call sinners, not to abide and rejoice in their auld iniquity, but to repentance; that is to an unfeigned dolour for the offences committed, and to a daily sorrowing, yea and hatred for that whilk resteth, with a hope of mercy and forgiveness of God by the redemption that is in Christ's blood.

*   *   *

It is a cross to me to remember how easily the adversary, wha is the accuser of our brethren, wounds you. Resist him, Mother, and he shall flee frae you; resist him, I say, in faith, and obey not the lusts of the flesh, and he shall be confounded and his darts quenched. 'There is no condemnation to them that are in Christ Jesus, that walk not after the flesh'; they walk after the flesh that, without fear or reverence to God, obeys the wicked appetites thereof, and studies by all means to fulfil the same, as God forbid that ye do.

Ye enquire, How can ye avoid the sentences pronounced against whoremongers, adulterers and such others? I answer, That if ye be such as obstinately continues in such iniquity, and purposeth not to avoid and abstain frae the same, then assuredly such sentences are spoken against you so long as that ye delight in that malignity; but if ye confess your sin, desiring deliverance therefrom, God is potent to remit the same. I regard not what sometimes ye have been, ('for sometimes we were darkness, but not light in the Lord') but what unfeignedly ye desire to be, that ye are in God's presence; for 'blessed are they' pronounced to be, by Jesus Christ, 'that hungers and thirsts after righteousness'; to whom is also made a promise that they shall be replenished. Ye cannot hunger and thirst for things that ye have abundantly, but for the things that ye lack and need. Abide, Mother, the time of harvest, before whilk must needs go the cold of winter, the temperate and unstable spring, and the fervent heat of summer; to be plain, ye must needs sow with tears or ye reap with gladness; sin must in you go before justice, death before life, weakness before strength, unstableness before stability, and bitterness before comfort. But in all these shall such as patiently will abide the Lord's deliverance, wha will come when least is our expectation, vanquish and triumph to his everlasting praise, Amen.

This Saturday at Newcastle, when my vocation calleth me to other labour; but God shall freely give what lacketh in me.

Your son,
John Knox

Laing III, pp 382-5
[spelling modernised]

XI

A DECLARATION
WHAT TRUE PRAYER IS

[*During his ministry in England, Knox prepared a short treatise on prayer for the benefit of 'the small and dispersed flock of Jesus Christ'. The following paragraphs are taken from it.*]

WHAT PRAYER IS.—Who will pray, must know and understand that Prayer is an earnest and familiar talking with God, to whom we declare our miseries, whose support and help we implore and desire in our adversities, and whom we laud and praise for our benefits received. So that Prayer containeth the exposition of our dolours [*ie* troubles] the desire of God's defence, and the praise of his magnificent name, as the Psalms of David clearly do teach.

* * *

WHY WE SHOULD PRAY, AND ALSO UNDERSTAND WHAT WE DO PRAY.—But men will object and say, Albeit we understand not what we pray, yet God understandeth, who knoweth the secrets of our hearts; he knoweth also what we need, although we expone not, or declare not, our necessities unto him. Sic men verily declare them selves never to have understanding what perfect prayer meant, not to what end Jesus Christ commandeth us to pray; whilk is First, That our hearts may be inflamed with continual fear, honour and love of God, to whom we run for support and help whensoever danger or necessity requireth; that we, so learning to notify our desires in his presence, he may teach us what is to be desired and what not. Secondly, That we knowing our petitions to be granted by God alone, to him only we must render and give laud and praise, and that we ever having his infinite goodness fixed in our minds, may constantly abide to receive that whilk with fervent prayer we desire.

* * *

PRIVATE PRAYER.—Private prayer, such as men secretly offer unto God by them selves, requires no special place; although that Jesus Christ commandeth when we pray to enter into our chamber, and to close the door, and so to pray secretly unto our Father. Whereby he would that we should choose to our prayers sic places as might offer least occasion to call us back from prayer; and also, that we should expel furth of our minds in time of our prayer, all vain cogitations. For otherwise Jesus Christ himself doth observe no special place of prayer: for we find him sometime pray in Mount Olivet, sometime in the Desert, sometime in the Temple, and in the Garden. And Peter coveteth to pray upon the top of the house. Paul prayed in prison and was heard of God. Who also commandeth men to pray in all places, lifting up to God pure and clean hands; as we find that the Prophets and most Holy men did, whensoever danger or necessity required.

APPOINTED PLACES TO PRAY IN, MAY NOT BE NEGLECTED.—But public and common prayers should be used in place appointed for the Assembly, from whence whosoever negligently extracteth themselves is in no wise excusable. I mean not, that to absent from that place is sin, because that place is more holy than another; for the whole earth created by

God is equally holy. But the promise made, that 'Where-soever two or three be gathered together in my name, there shall I be in the midst of them,' condemneth all such as contemneth the congregation gathered in his name. But mark well the word 'gathered'; I mean not to hear piping, singing, or playing; not to patter upon beads, or books whereof they have no understanding; nor to commit idolatry, honouring that for God whilk is no God in deed. For with such will I neither join my self in common prayer, nor in receiving external sacraments; for in so doing I should affirm their superstition and abominable idolatry, whilk I, by God's grace, never will do, neither counsel other to do, to the end.

WHAT IT IS TO BE GATHERED IN THE NAME OF CHRIST.—This congregation whilk I mean, should be gathered in the name of Jesus Christ, that is, to laud and magnify God the Father, for the infinite benefits they had received by his only Son our Lord. In this congregation should be distributed the mystical and last Supper of Jesus Christ without superstition, or any more ceremonies than he him self used and his Apostles after him. And in distribution thereof, in this congregation should inquisition be made of the poor among them, and support provided, while the time of their next convention, and it should be distributed amongst them. Also in this congregation should be made common prayers, such as all men hearing might understand; that the hearts of all, subscribing to the voice of one, might, with unfeigned and fervent mind, say, Amen.

Laing III, pp 83,85,102-3
{spelling modernised}

XII

LETTER
TO MARJORY BOWES

[The following letter, written probably in 1554, was, it seems, Knox's first letter to his fiancée.]

DEARLY beloved Sister in the common faith of Jesus our Saviour:

The place of John, forbidding us to salute such as bringeth not the wholesome doctrine, admonisheth us what danger cometh by false teachers, even the destruction of body and soul. Wherefore the Spirit of God willeth us to be so careful to avoid the company of all that teaches doctrine contrary to the truth of Christ, that we communicate with them in nothing that may appear to maintain or defend them in their corrupt opinion. For he that bids them Godspeed, communicates with their sin; that is, he that appears, by keeping them company, or assisting unto them in their proceedings, to favour their doctrine, is guilty before God of their iniquity, both because he doth confirm them in their error by his silence, and also confirms others to credit their doctrine, because he oppones not himself thereto. And so to bid them Godspeed is not to speak unto them commonly, as we, for civil honesty, to men unknown, but it is, after we have heard their false doctrine, to be conversant with them, and so entreat them as they had not offended in their doctrine. The place of James teaches us, beloved Sister, that in Jesus Christ all that unfeignedly profess him are equal before him, and

that riches nor worldly honours are nothing regarded in his
sight; and therefore would the Spirit of God, speaking in the
Apostle, that such as are true Christians should have more
respect to the spiritual gifts wherewith God had doted his
messengers, nor to external riches, whilk oftimes the wicked
possesses, the having whereof makes man neither noble
nor godly, albeit so judge the blind affections of men. The
Apostle damneth such as prefers a man with a golden chain
to the poor; but hereof I will speak no more.

The Spirit of God shall instruct your heart what is most
comfortable to the troubled conscience of your Mother, and
pray earnestly that so may be. Where the adversary objects,
She ought not think wicked thoughts; answer thereto, That is
true, but seeing this our nature is corrupted with sin, whilk
entered by his suggestion, it must think and work wickedly
by his assaults; but he shall bear the condign punishment
thereof, because by him sin first entered, and also by him it
doth continue whilst this carcase be resolved. And where he
inquires, What Christ is; answer, He is the seed of the woman
promised by God to break down the serpent's head, whilk
he hath done already, in him self appearing in this our flesh,
subject to all passions that may fall in this our nature, only
sin excepted; and after the death suffered, he hath, by power
of his Godhead, risen again triumphant victor over death,
hell and sin, not to him self, for thereto was he no debtor,
but for such as thirsts salvation by him only, whom he may
no more lose, nor he may cease to be the Son of God and the
saviour of the world. And where he would persuade that
she is contrary the word thereto, he lies according to his
nature, wherein there is no truth; for if she were contrary the
word, or denied it, to what effect so earnestly should she
desire the company of such as teacheth and professeth it?
There is no doubt but he, as he is the accuser of all God's

elect, studieth to trouble her conscience, that according to her desire she may not rest in Jesus our Lord. Be vigilant in prayer.

I think this be the first Letter that ever I wrote to you.

In great haste, your Brother,

John Knox

Laing III, pp 394f
{spelling modernised}

XIII

AVOIDING IDOLATRY

[*The following paragraphs are taken from 'A Godly Letter of Warning or Admonition to the faithful in London, Newcastle and Berwick', published in 1554.*]

O DEARLY Beloved, if we will stand in league with God, and be accounted the children of faith, we must follow the footsteps of Abraham who, at God's commandment, left his native country, because it was defiled with idolatry. God gave to him but one commandment, saying, 'Pass out of thy Father's house,' and he, without further reasoning, did obey. And alas! shall not so many precepts as be given to flee and avoid idolatry, move us, seeing that God shows him self so offended with idolaters, that he commands all such to be slain without mercy.

But now shall some demand, What then? Shall we go and slay all idolaters? That were the office, dear brethren, of every Civil Magistrate within his realm. But of you is required only to avoid participation and company of their abominations, as well in body as in soul; as David and Paul plainly teaches unto you. David in his exile, in the midst of idolaters, sayeth, 'I will not offer their drink offerings of blood, neither yet will I take their name in my mouth.' And Paul says, 'Ye may not be partakers of the Lord's table and of the table of the Devils, ye may not drink the Lord's cup and the cup of the Devils.'

* * *

It shall nothing excuse us to say, We trust not in Idols, for so will every Idolater allege; but if either you or they in God's honour do anything contrary to God's Word, you show your self to put your trust in somewhat else besides God, and so are you idolaters. Mark, Brethren, that many maketh an idol of their own wisdom or fantasy: more trusting to that which they think good, nor unto God, who plainly sayeth, not that things which seemeth good in thy eyes, do unto thy God, but what thy Lord God hath commanded them.

* * *

Now resteth it to show, that true faith and the confession of the same, necessarily requires that body and soul be clean from idolatry. It is not needful that I labour in the first seeing, that almost no man denyeth it: But a perfect faith, as it purgeth the heart, so does it remove, and cast out from the same superstition and abominable idolatry. But whether an inward faith requireth an external confession, and that the body avoid idolatry, some perchance may doubt. To the one part the Apostle answers, saying, 'The heart believes unto Justice, but by the mouth is confession to Salvation.' And David likewise, 'I have believed and therefore have I spoken; but I was sore troubled.' As David would say, I could not conceal the confession of my faith, howbeit trouble did ensue the same. In this place, the voice of the Holy Spirit joineth together faith, as things that be inseparable the one from the other; an therefore dare I not take upon me to dissever them; But must say, that where true faith is, that there is also confession of the same when time and necessity requireth; and that where confession is absent, that their faith is asleep, or else (whilk more is to be feared) far from home. For like as eating, drinking, speaking, moving, and other operations of a living body, declares the body to be alive, and not to be dead; so does confession, in time convenient, declare the faith to be living. And as impotence to do any of the fore-named offices of the body, declares the same either to be dead, or else shortly and assuredly to die; so like confession not given in due time makes manifest that the soul has no life by true faith.

* * *

Hereof it is plain, that requiring you not to profane your bodies with idolatry, I require no more nor God's most sacred Scriptures by plain precepts and examples teaches unto us. And of every man, and at all times, I require not so muckle, for I constrain no man to go to idolaters in the time of their idolatry, and to say, Your Gods made neither Heaven nor Earth, and therefore shall they perish, and ye with them, for all your worshipping is abominable idolatry. But I require only that we absent our bodies (called of the Apostle the Temple of the Holy Ghost) from all such diabolical conventions, whilk if we do, is both profitable and necessary, no less to ourselves than to our posterity.

Laing III, pp 194,196,197-8,202-3
{spelling modernised}

XIV

THE DUTY
OF A PREACHER

[These paragraphs are taken from a pamphlet entitled 'A Faithful Admonition to the Professors of God's Truth in England', published in 1554.]

SOME complained in those days, That the preachers were indiscreet persons, yea, and some called them railers, and worse, because they spake against the manifest iniquity of men, and especially of those that then were placed in authority, as well in the Court, as in other offices universally throughout the Realm, both in cities, towns and villages. And among other, peradventure, my rude plainness displeased some, who did complain that rashly I did speak of men's faults; so that all men might know and perceive of whom I meant.

But alas! this day my conscience accuseth me, that I spake not so plainly as my duty was to have done: for I ought to have said to the wicked man expressedly by his name, 'Thou shalt die the death.' For I find Jeremiah the prophet to have done to Pashur the high priest and to Zedekiah the king. And not only him, but also Elijah, Elisha, Micah, Amos, Daniel, Christ Jesus himself, and after him his Apostles, expressedly to have named the blood-thirsty tyrants abominable idolaters, and dissembling hypocrites of their day. If that we the preachers within the Realm of England were appointed by God to be the salt of the earth (as his other messengers were before us) alas! why

held we back the salt where manifest corruption did appear?
(I accuse none but my self). The blind love that I did bear to
this my wicked carcase, was the chief cause that I was not
fervent and faithful enough in that behalf: for I had no will
to provoke the hatred of all men against me; and therefore so
touched I the vices of men in the presence of the greatest,
that they might see themselves to be offenders; (I dare not
say that I was the greatest flatterer); but yet, nevertheless, I
would not be seen to proclaim manifest war against the
manifest wicked; whereof unfeignedly I ask my God mercy.

Laing III, p 269-70
{spelling modernised}

XV

THE FIRST TEMPTATION
OF CHRIST

[The following paragraphs are taken from an incomplete sermon on the Temptations of Christ which was published in London in 1583, but probably first preached in Edinburgh in 1556.]

MATTHEW IV, verse the 4th, But he, answering said, It is written, Man liveth not by bread only, but by every word whilk proceedeth out of the mouth of God.

BUT that ye may the better understand the meaning of Christ's answer, we will phrase and repeat it over in more words. 'Thou labourest Satan (will Christ say) to bring in my heart a doubt and suspicion of my Father's promise, whilk was openly proclaimed in my baptism, by reason of my hunger, and that I lack all carnal provision. Thou art bold to affirm that God taketh no care over me: but thou art a deceitful and false corrupt sophister, and thy argument is vain and full of blasphemies; for thou bindest God's love, mercy and providence to the having or wanting of corporal provision, whilk no part of God's Scriptures do teach us, but rather they express contrary. As it is written, 'Man liveth not by bread only, but by every word that proceedeth from the mouth of God'; that is, the very life and felicity of man consisteth not in abundance of corporal things, for the possession and having of them maketh no man blessed nor happy; neither shall the lack of them be the cause of his final misery; but the very life of man consisteth in God, and in his promises pronounced by his own mouth, unto the whilk whoso cleaveth and sticketh unfeignedly, shall live the life everlasting.

'And although all creatures in earth forsake him, yet shall not his corporal life perish till the time appointed by God approach: For God hath means to feed, preserve and maintain, unknown to man's reason, and contrary to the common course of nature: He fed his people Israel in the desert forty years, without the provision of man. He preserved Jonah in the whale's belly; and maintained and kept the bodies of the three children in the furnace of fire. Reason and the natural man could have seen nothing in these cases but destruction and death, and could have judged nothing, but that God had cast away the care of these his creatures, and yet was his providence most vigilant towards them in the extremity of their dangers, from whilk he did so deliver them, and in the midst of them did so assist them, that his glory, whilk is his mercy and goodness, did more appear and shine after their troubles than it could have done if they had not fallen in them. And therefore I measure not the truth and favour of God, by having or by lacking of corporal necessities, but by the promise that he hath made to me: as He him self is immutable, so is his word and promise constant, whilk I believe, and to whilk I stick and do cleave, what ever can come externally to the body.'

* * *

Thus are we taught, I say, by Christ Jesus, to repulse Satan and his assaults by the Word of God, and to apply the examples of his mercies, whilk he hath showed to others before us, to our own souls in the hour of temptation, and in the time of our troubles.   *Laing IV, pp 110-13* {spelling modernised}

XVI

THE DAILY EXERCISE
OF GOD'S MOST HOLY
AND SACRED WORD

[Just before he left Scotland in 1556, Knox prepared a 'Letter of Wholesome Counsel how to behave ourselves in the midst of this wicked generation', from which the following paragraphs are taken.]

NOT so much to instruct you, as to leave with you (dearly beloved Brethren) some testimony of my love, I have thought good to communicate with you, in these few lines, my weak counsel, how I would ye should behave your selves in the midst of this wicked generation, touching the exercise of God's most sacred and holy Word, without which, neither shall knowledge increase, godliness appear, nor fervency continue amongst you. For as the Word is the beginning of life spiritual, without which all flesh is dead in God's presence, and the lantern to our feet, without the brightness whereof all the posterity of Adam doth walk in darkness; and as it is the foundation of faith, without which no man understandeth the good will of God, so it is also the only organ and instrument which God useth to strengthen the weak, to comfort the afflicted, to reduce to mercy by repentance such as have slidden, and, finally, to preserve and keep the very life of the soul in all assaults and temptations. And thereof, if that ye desire your knowledge to be increased, your faith to be confirmed, your conscience to be quieted and comforted, or, finally, your soul to be preserved in life, let your exercise be frequent in the law of your Lord God.

* * *

Now if the Law, which by reason of our weakness can work
nothing but wrath and anger, was so effectual, that remem-
bered and rehearsed of purpose to do it, it brought to the
people a corporal benediction, what shall we say that the
glorious Gospel of Christ Jesus doth work, so that with
reverence it be entreated? S. Paul calleth it the sweet odour of
life to those that shall receive life, borrowing his similitude
of odouriferous herbs or precious ointments, whose nature is,
the more that they be touched or moved, to send forth their
odour more pleasant and delectable: Even such, dear Brethren
is the blessed Evangel of our Lord Jesus; for the more that it
be entreated, the more comfortable and puissant is it to such
as do hear, read, or exercise the same.

* * *

But if such men, as having liberty to read and exercise them
selves in God's holy Scriptures, and yet begin to weary, because from time to time they read but one thing, I ask, Why
weary they not also every day to eat bread? Every day to
drink wine? Every day to behold the brightness of the sun?
And to use the rest of God's creatures, which every day do
keep their own substance, course and nature? They shall
answer, I trust, Because such creatures have a strength to
preserve the life. O miserable creatures! Who dare attribute
more power and strength to corruptible creatures in nourishing
and preserving the mortal carcase, than to the eternal Word
of God in the nourishment of the soul, which is immortal!

* * *

And therefore, dear Brethren, if that ye look for a life to come, of necessity it is that ye exercise your selves in the book of the Lord your God. Let no day slip or want some comfort received from the mouth of God. Open your ears, and he will speak even pleasant things to your heart. Close not your eyes, but diligently let them behold what portion of substance is left to you within your Father's testament. Let your tongues learn to praise the gracious goodness of Him, whose mere mercy hath called you from darkness to light, and from death to life.

Laing IV, pp 133-7
{spelling modernised}

XVII

FAMILY AND
CORPORATE WORSHIP

[The following paragraphs are also taken from 'A Letter of Whole-some Counsel'.]

BRETHREN, ye are ordained of God to rule your own houses in his true fear and according to his Word. Within your own houses, I say, in some cases, ye are bishops and kings; your wife, children, servants, and family are your bishopric and charge; of you it shall be required how carefully and diligently ye have always instructed them in God's true knowledge, how that ye have studied in them to plant virtue and repress vice. And therefore, I say, ye must make them partakers in reading, exhorting, and in making common prayers, which I would in every house were used once a day at least. But above all things, dear Brethren, study to practise in life that which the Word of God commandeth, and then be you assured that ye shall never hear nor read the same without fruit. And thus much for the exercises within your house.

Considering that Saint Paul calleth the congregation 'the body of Christ' whereof every one of us is a member, teaching us thereby that no member is of sufficiency to sustain and feed itself without the help and support of another; I think it necessary for the conference of Scriptures, assemblies of brethren be had. The order therein to be observed is expressed by S. Paul, and therefore need not I to use many words in that behalf; only willing, that when ye convene or come together, which I would were once a week, that your beginning

84

should be from confession of your offences, and invocation of the Spirit of the Lord Jesus to assist you in all your godly enterprises. And then let some place of Scripture be plainly and distinctly read, so much as shall be thought sufficient for one day or time; which ended, if any brother have exhortation, question, or doubt, let him not fear to speak or move the same, so that he do it with moderation, either to edify or be edified. And hereof I doubt not but great profit shall shortly ensue; for, first, by hearing, reading, and conferring the Scriptures in the assembly, the whole body of the Scriptures of God shall become familiar, the judgments and spirits of men shall be tried, their patience and modesty shall be known; and, finally, their gifts and utterance shall appear. Multiplication of words, prolixed interpretations, and wilfulness in reasoning, is to be avoided at all times, and in all places, but chiefly in the congregation where nothing ought to be respected except the glory of God, and comfort or edification of brethren.

If any thing occur within the text, or else arise in reasoning, whilk your judgment can not resolve or capacities apprehend, let the same be noted and put in writing before ye dismiss the congregation, that when God shall offer unto you any interpreter, your doubts being noted and known, may have the more expedite resolution; or else that when ye shall have occasion to write to such as with whom ye would communicate your judgments, your letters may signify and declare your increasing desire that ye have of God and of his true religion; and they, I doubt not, according to their talents, will endeavour and bestow their faithful labours to satisfy your godly petitions.

* * *

Like as your assemblies ought to begin with confession and invocation of God's Holy Spirit, so would I that they were finished with thanksgiving and common prayers for princes, rulers and magistrates; for the liberty and free passage of Christ's Evangel, for the comfort and deliverance of our afflicted brethren in all places now persecuted, but most cruelly within the realm of France and England; and for such other things as the Spirit of the Lord Jesus shall teach unto you to be profitable, either to your selves, or to your brethren wheresoever they be.

Laing IV, pp 137-9
{spelling modernised}

XVIII

THE ORDER OF THE ELECTION
OF ELDERS AND DEACONS

[In his 'History of the Reformation in Scotland', Knox gives this account of how his advice in the conduct of Privy Kirks was followed.]

THE ORDER OF THE ELECTION OF ELDERS AND DEACONS IN THE PRIVY KIRK OF EDINBURGH, IN THE BEGINNING, WHEN AS YET THERE WAS NO PUBLIC FACE OF A KIRK, NOR OPEN ASSEMBLIES, BUT SECRET AND PRIVY CONVENTIONS IN HOUSES, OR IN THE FIELDS.

BEFORE that there was any public face of a true Religion within this Realm, it pleased God of his great mercy, to illuminate the hearts of many private persons, so that they did perceive and understand the abuses that were in the Papistical Kirk, and thereupon withdrew themselves from participation of their idolatry. And because the Spirit of God will never suffer his own to be idle and void of all religion, men began to exercise themselves in reading of the Scriptures secretly within their own houses; and variety of persons could not be kept in good obedience and honest fame, without Overseers, Elders, and Deacons: And so began that small flock to put themselves in such order, as if Christ Jesus had plainly triumphed in the midst of them by the power of his Evangel. And they did elect some to occupy the supreme place of exhortation and reading, some to be Elders and

helpers unto them, for the oversight of the flock: And some
to be Deacons for the collection of alms to be distributed to
the poor of their own body. Of this small beginning is that
Order, which now God of his great mercy has given unto us
publicly within this Realm.

Dickinson II, p 277

XIX

THE DUTY
OF SPEAKING OUT

[The following paragraphs are taken from the Preface to the 'First Blast of the Trumpet against the Monstrous Regiment of Women'.]

THE Kingdom apertaineth to our God.

Wonder it is, that amongst so many pregnant wits as the Isle of Great Britain hath produced, so many godly and zealous preachers as England did sometime nourish, and amongst so many learned, and men of grave judgment, as this day by Jezebel [*ie* Queen Mary Tudor] are exiled, none is found so stout of courage, so faithful to God, nor loving to their native country, that they dare admonish the inhabitants of that Isle, how abominable before God is the Empire or Rule of a wicked woman.

* * *

We in this our miserable age are bound to admonish the world, and the tyrants thereof, of their sudden destruction, to assure them, and to cry unto them, whether they list to hear or not, 'That the blood of the Saints, which by them is shed, continually crieth and craveth vengeance in the presence of the Lord of Hosts'. And further, it is our duty to open the truth revealed unto us, unto the ignorant and blind world; unless that to our own condemnation we list to wrap up and hide the talent committed to our charge. I am assured, that God hath revealed to some in this our age, that it is more than a monster in nature that a Woman shall reign and have empire above Man. And yet with us all there is such silence, as if God therewith were nothing offended.

The natural man, enemy to God, shall find, I know, many causes why no such doctrine ought to be published in those our dangerous days. First, for that it may seem to tend to sedition. Secondarily, it shall be dangerous, not only to the writer or publisher, but also to all such as shall read the writings, or favour this truth spoken: And last, It shall not amend the chief offenders, partly because it shall never come to their ears, and partly because they will not be admonished in such cases.

I answer, If any of these be a sufficient reason, that a truth known shall be concealed, then were the ancient Prophets of God very fools, who did not better provide for their own quietness, than to hazard their lives for rebuking of vices, and for the opening of such crimes as were not known to the world. And Christ Jesus did injury to his Apostles, commanding them to preach repentance and remission of sins in his name to every realm and nation. And Paul did not understand his own liberty, when he cried, 'Woe be to me, if I preach not the Evangel!' If fear, I say, of persecution, of slander, or of any inconvenience before named, might have excused and discharged the servants of God from plainly rebuking the sins of the world, just cause had every one of them to have ceased from their office. For suddenly their doctrine was accused by terms of sedition, of new learning, and of treason. Persecution and vehement trouble did shortly come upon the professors with the preachers: Kings, Princes, and worldly Rulers did conspire against God and against his anointed Christ Jesus. But what? Did any of these move the Prophets and Apostles to faint in their vocation? No. But by the resistance which the Devil made to them by his supposts [*ie* supporters] were they the more inflamed to publish the truth revealed unto them; and to witness with their blood, that grievous condemnation and God's heavy vengeance should follow the proud contempt of graces offered. The fidelity, bold courage, and constancy of those that are passed before us, ought to provoke us to follow their footsteps, unless we look for another Kingdom than Christ hath promised to such as persevere in profession of his name to the end.

Laing IV, pp 365-368
{spelling modernised}

XX

DEBORAH

[In this extract from the 'First Blast of the Trumpet against the Monstrous Regiment of Women', Knox replies to those who suggest that Deborah, who judged Israel, is a precedent of rule by a woman.]

SUCH as have more pleasure in light than in darkness may clearly perceive that Deborah did usurp no such power nor authority as our Queens do this day claim; but that she was indued with the spirit of wisdom, of knowledge, and of the true fear of God, and by the same she judged the facts of the rest of the people. She rebuked their defection and idolatry, yea, and also did redress to her power the injuries that were done by man to man. But all this, I say, she did by the spiritual sword, that is, by the Word of God, and not by any temporal regiment or authority which she did usurp over Israel, in which, I suppose, at that time there was no lawful Magistrate, by the reason of their great affliction; for so witnesseth the history, saying, 'And Ehud being dead, the Lord sold Israel in to the hand of Jabin, King of Canaan': and he by Sisera his captain afflicted Israel greatly the space of twenty years. And Deborah her self, in her song of thanks giving, confesseth, that before she did arise mother in Israel, and in the days of Jael, there was nothing but confusion and trouble.

If any stick to the term, alleging that the Holy Ghost saith 'that she judged Israel' let them understand, that neither doth the Hebrew word, neither yet the Latin, always signify

Civil judgment, or the execution of the Temporall sword, but most commonly is taken in the sense which we have before expressed. For of Christ it is said, 'He shall judge many nations' and that 'He shall pronounce judgment to the Gentiles'; and yet it is evident that he was no minister of the temporal sword. God commandeth Jerusalem and Judah to judge betwixt him and his vineyard, and yet he appointed not them all to be Civil magistrates. To Ezekiel it is said, 'Shalt thou not judge them, Son of man?' And after, 'Thou Son of Man, shalt thou not judge? Shalt thou not judge, I say, the city of blood?' And also, 'Behold I shall judge betwixt beast and beast.' And such places, in great number are to be found throughout the whole Scriptures.

* * *

And so I doubt not but Deborah judged, what time Israel had declined from God, rebuking their defection, and exhorting them to repentance, without usurpation of any civil authority: And if the people gave unto her for a time any reverence or honour, as her godliness and happy counsel did well deserve, yet was it no such empire as our monsters claim; for which of her sons or nearest kinsmen left she ruler and judge in Israel after her? The Holy Ghost expresseth no such thing: whereof it is evident, that by her example God offereth no occasion to establish any regiment of Women above men, realms, and nations.

Laing IV, pp 407-409

XXI

THE RIGHT AND DUTY
TO DEMAND REFORM

[*The following paragraphs are taken from 'A Letter addressed to the Commonalty of Scotland'.*]

TRUE it is, that Mahomet pronounced this sentence, that no man should, in pain of death, dispute or reason of the ground of his religion. Which law, to this day, by the art of Satan, is yet observed amongst the Turks, to their mortal blindness and horrible blaspheming of Christ Jesus, and of his true religion. And from Mahomet (or rather from Satan, father of all lies) hath the Pope and his rabble learned this former lesson, to wit, that their religion should not be disputed upon; but what the fathers have believed, that ought and must the children approve. And in so devising, Satan lacked not his foresight: For no one thing hath more established the kingdom of that Roman Antichrist than this most wicked Decree, to wit, That no man was permitted to reason of his power, or to call his laws in doubt. This thing is most assured, that whensoever the Papistical religion shall come to examination, it shall be found to have no other ground than hath the religion of Mahomet, to wit, man's invention, device and dreams, overshadowed with some colour of God's Word.

And therefore, Brethren, seeing that the Religion is as the stomach to the body, which, if it be corrupted, doth infect the whole members, it is necessary that the same be examined, and if it be found replenished with pestilent humours (I mean with the fantasies of men), then of necessity it is that those be purged, else shall your bodies and souls perish for ever. For of this I would ye were most certainly persuaded, that a corrupt religion defileth the whole life of man, appear it never so holy.

Neither would I that ye should esteem the Reformation and care of Religion less to appertain to you, because ye are no Kings, Rulers, Judges, Nobles, nor in authority. Beloved Brethren, ye are God's creatures, created and formed to his own image and similitude, for whose redemption was shed the most precious blood of the only beloved Son of God, to whom he hath commanded his gospel and glad-tidings to be preached, and for whom he hath prepared the heavenly inheritance, so that ye will not obstinately refuse and disdainfully contemn the means, which he hath appointed to obtain the same, to wit, his blessed Evangel, which now he offereth unto you, to the end that ye may be saved. For the gospel and glad-tidings of the kingdom truly preached, is the power of God to the salvation of every believer, which to credit and receive, you, the Commonalty, are no less addebted than be your Rulers and Princes. For albeit God hath put and ordained distinction and difference betwixt the King and subjects, betwixt the Rulers and the common people in the regiment and administration of Civil policies, yet in the hope of the life to come he hath made all equal.

*   *   *

And thus if ye look for the life everlasting, ye must try if ye stand in faith; and if ye would be assured of a true and lively faith, ye must needs have Christ Jesus truly preached unto you. And this is the cause, dear Brethren, that so oft I repeat, and so constantly I affirm, that to you it doth no less appertain, than to your King or Princes, to provide that Christ Jesus be truly preached amongst you, seeing that without his true knowledge can neither of you both attain to salvation.

Laing IV. pp 525-8
{spelling modernised}

XXII

PREDESTINATION

[The following paragraph is taken from a lengthy treatise on Predestination written by Knox in Geneva in 1558 but not published until 1560. It is in the form of a reply to an Anabaptist.]

YE are so inconstant, now granting Predestination to be the free and mere gift of God, without any condition of our works, and immediately after ascribing it to our obedience, and walking in the way that leadeth to life. In this your inconstancy, I say, I can not tell how to handle you. One thing I see, to my great comfort, that the glory of Christ Jesus is so manifest, and the power of his truth so invincible, that he will reign in the midst of his enemies. The devils themselves must acknowledge and openly confess that he is Lord, and the only Son of the living Father; and the adversaries of his truth, even when they fight most outrageously against the same, are compelled to give testimony to it, as you do here in divers places; as when ye say, 'It followeth not, that because we must walk in the way that leadeth to life, that therefore, for walking in the way of salvation, we are chosen, and (as you write) accepted.' But because, I say, that your inconstancy doth straight carry you to denial of this, I can the less credit that this be a true confession, proceeding from an unfeigned heart, but rather that it is the mighty power of the verity, which (will ye, nill ye) compelleth your mouths to give witnessing, upon her part, against yourselves. God grant I may be deceived in this my judgment;

for him I take to record, that I am no otherwise enemy to any of you, than in so far ye declare yourselves manifest enemies to the free grace of God, and to the glory of the eternal Son of the eternal Father of Christ Jesus, our Lord and only Saviour.

Laing V, pp 203 f
{spelling modernised}

XXIII

THE POWER
OF THE WORD OF GOD

[*The following paragraphs are taken from Knox's treatise on Predestination.*]

THE Lord himself saith unto Jeremiah, 'Behold, I have put my words in thy mouth, and I have ordained thee above nations and kingdoms, that thou mayest root out, destroy and scatter, and that thou mayest also build up and plant.' And unto Paul it was said, 'And now I shall deliver thee from the nations to the which I send thee, that thou mayest open the eyes of those that be blind, that they may convert from darkness unto light, and from the power of Satan unto God.' These words do witness, that the effectual power of God doth work with the word which he putteth in the mouths of his true messengers, insomuch, that either it doth edify, lighten or mollify to salvation; or else it doth destroy, darken and harden. For the Word of God is of the nature of Christ Jesus; and he is not only come to illuminate and to raise up, but also to make blind and beat down; as he himself doth witness, saying, 'I am come to judgment into this world, that those that see not shall see, and that those that see shall be blind.' And Simeon saith, 'Behold this is he that is put in resurrection and in ruin of many in Israel'; insomuch 'that upon whom that stone of offence falleth, it shall burst him to powder.'

And therefore, we can not admit that the ministry of his

blessed Word, preached or published by his faithful messengers be nothing else but a simple declaration what men be. No; we know that it is the power of God to salvation of all those that believe; that the message of reconciliation is put in their mouths; that the word which they preach hath such efficacy and strength, that it divideth asunder the joints and sinews, the bones from the marrow; that the weapons of their warfare are not carnal, but are power in God to the beating down of all strongholds, by the which the true messengers beat down all counsels, and all height which is raised up against the knowledge of God; by the which also they lead into bondage all cogitations, to obey Christ. We know further, that they have vengeance in readiness against all inobedience; that fire passeth forth of their mouths which devoureth their enemies; that they have power to shut the heaven, that rain descend not in the days of their prophecy. That God's power, both in the one sort and in the other, is contained with his Word, even preached, pronounced, and fore-spoken by his messengers, do all examples in God's Scriptures witness.

Laing V, pp 385f
{spelling modernised}

XXIV

A PRAYER
FOR THE WHOLE ESTATE
OF CHRIST'S CHURCH

[This prayer from the 'Forme of Prayers' 1556 was intended to be used after the Sermon. With adaptations, it was later used in Scotland in various editions of the 'Book of Common Order' including that of 1940.]

ALMIGHTY and most merciful Father, we humbly submit our selves, and fall down before thy Majesty, beseeching thee from the bottom of our hearts, that this seed of thy word, now sown amongst us, may take such deep root, that neither the burning heat of persecution cause it to wither, neither the thorny cares of this life do choke it, but that as seed sown in good ground, it may bring forth thirty, sixty, and an hundred fold, as thy heavenly wisdom hath appointed. And because we have need continually to crave many things at thy hands, we humbly beseech thee, O heavenly Father, to grant us thy Holy Spirit to direct our petitions, that they may proceed from such a fervent mind as may be agreeable to thy most blessed will.

And seeing that our infirmity is able to do nothing without thy help, and that thou art not ignorant with how many and great temptations, we poor wretches are on every side inclosed and compassed, let thy strength, O Lord, sustain our weakness, that we being defended with the force of thy grace, nay be safely preserved against all assaults of Satan, who goeth about continually like a roaring lion, seeking to devour us. Increase our faith, O merciful Father, that we not swerve at any time from thy heavenly word, but augment in us hope and love, with a careful keeping of all thy commandments, that no hardness of heart, no hypocrisy, no concupiscence of the eyes, nor enticements of the world, do draw us away from thy obedience. And seeing we live now in these most perilous times, let thy Fatherly providence defend us against the violence of all our enemies, which do everywhere pursue us; but chiefly against the wicked rage and furious uproars of that Romish idol, enemy to thy Christ.

Furthermore, for as much as by thy holy Apostle we be taught to make our prayers and supplications for all men, we pray not only for our selves here present, but beseech thee also, to reduce all such as be yet ignorant, from the miserable captivity of blindness and error, to the pure understanding and knowledge of thy heavenly truth, that we all, with one consent and unity of minds, may worship thee our only God and Saviour. And that all pastors, shepherds, and ministers, to whom thou has committed the dispensation of thy holy Word, and charge of thy chosen people, may both in their life and doctrine be found faithful, setting only before their eyes thy glory; and that by them, all poor sheep which wander and go astray, may be gathered and brought home to thy fold.

Moreover, because the hearts of rulers are in thy hands, we beseech thee to direct and govern the hearts of all kings, princes, and magistrates to whom thou hast committed the sword; especially, O Lord, according to our bounden duty, we beseech thee to maintain and increase the honourable estate of this city, in whose defence we are received, the magistrates, the council, and all the whole body of this commonweal: Let thy Fatherly favour so preserve them, and thy

Holy Spirit so govern their hearts, that they may in such sort execute their office, that thy religion may be purely maintained, manners reformed, and sin punished according to the precise rule of thy holy Word.

And for that we be all members of the mystical body of Christ Jesus, we make our requests unto thee, O heavenly Father, for all such as are afflicted with any kind of cross or tribulation, as war, plague, famine, sickness, poverty, imprisonment, persecution, banishment, or any other kind of thy rods, whether it be calamity of body, or vexation of mind, that it would please thee to give them patience and constancy, till thou send them full deliverance of all their troubles. And as we bound to love and honour our parents, kinsfolks, friends and country, so we most humbly beseech thee to show thy pity upon our miserable country of England, which once, through thy mercy, was called to liberty, and now for their and our sins, is brought unto most vile slavery and Babylonical bondage.

Root out from thence, O Lord, all ravening wolves, which to fill their bellies destroy thy flock. And show thy great mercies upon those our brethren which are persecuted, cast in prison, and daily condemned to death for the testimony of thy truth. And though they be utterly destitute of all man's aid, yet let thy sweet comfort never depart from them, but so inflame their hearts with thy Holy Spirit, that they may boldly and cheerfully abide such trial as thy godly wisdom shall appoint. So that at length, as well by their death as by their life, the Kingdom of thy dear Son Jesus Christ may increase and shine through all the world. In whose name we make our humble petitions unto thee, as he hath taught us.

Our Father which are in heaven, *etc.*

Almighty and ever living God, vouchsafe, we beseech

thee, to grant us perfect continuance in thy lively faith, augmenting the same in us daily, till we grow to the full measure of our perfection in Christ, whereof we make our confession, saying,

I believe in God, *etc.*

Laing IV, pp 182-5
{spelling modernised}

XXV

Exhortation
at The Lord's Supper

[Taken from the 'Forme of Prayers' 1556.]

DEARLY beloved in the Lord, forasmuch as we be now assembled to celebrate the holy Communion of the body and blood of our Saviour Christ, let us consider these words of S. Paul, how he exhorteth all persons diligently to try and examine them selves before they presume to eat of that bread and drink of that cup. For as the benefit is great, if with a truly penitent heart and lively faith we receive that holy sacrament, (for then we spiritually eat the flesh of Christ and drink his blood, then we dwell in Christ and Christ in us, we be one with Christ and Christ with us,) so is the danger great if we receive the same unworthily, for then we be guilty of the body and blood of Christ our Saviour, we eat and drink our own damnation, not considering the Lord's body; we kindle God's wrath against us, and provoke him to plague us with diverse diseases and sundry kinds of death.

Therefore if any of you be a blasphemer of God, an hinderer or slanderer of his Word, an adulterer, or be in malice or envy, or in any other grievous crime, bewail your sins, and come not to this holy Table, lest after the taking of this holy sacrament, the Devil enter into you as he entered into Judas, and fill you full of all iniquities, and bring you to destruction both of body and soul.

Judge therefore your selves, Brethren, that ye be not judged of the Lord; repent you truly for your sins past, and have a lively and steadfast faith in Christ our Saviour, seeking only your salvation in the merits of his death and passion, from henceforth refusing and forgetting all malice and debate, with full purpose to live in brotherly amity and godly conversation all the days of your life.

And albeit we feel in ourselves much frailty and wretchedness, as that we have not our faith so perfect and constant as we ought, being many times ready to distrust God's goodness through our corrupt nature, and also that we are not so thoroughly given to serve God, neither have so fervent a zeal to set forth his glory as our duty requireth, feeling still such rebellion in our selves, that we have need daily to fight against the lusts of our flesh; yet, nevertheless, seeing that our Lord hath dealt thus mercifully with us, that he hath printed his Gospel in our hearts, so that we are preserved from falling into desperation and misbelief; and seeing also he hath indued us with a will and desire to renounce and withstand our own affections, with a longing for his righteousness and the keeping of his commandments, we may be now right well assured, that those defaults and manifold imperfections in us, shall be no hindrance at all against us, to cause him not to accept and impute us as worthy to come to his spiritual Table. For the end of our coming thither is not to make protestation that we are upright and just in our lives, but contrary wise, we come to seek our life and perfection in Jesus Christ, acknowledging in the mean time, that we of our selves be the children of wrath and damnation.

Let us consider, then, that this Sacrament is a singular medicine for all poor sick creatures, a comfortable help to weak souls, and that the Lord requireth no other worthiness on our part, but that we unfeignedly acknowledge our naughtiness and imperfection. Then to the end that we may be worthy partakers of his merits and most comfortable benefits (which is the true eating of his flesh and drinking of his blood,) let us not suffer our minds to wander about the consideration of these earthly and corruptible things (which we see present to our eyes, and feel with our hands,) to seek Christ bodily present in them, as if he were enclosed in the bread or wine, or as if these elements were turned and changed into the substance of his flesh and blood. For the only way to dispose our souls to receive nourishment, relief, and quickening of his substance, is to lift up our minds by faith above all things worldly and sensible, and thereby to enter into heaven, that we may find and receive Christ, where he dwelleth undoubtedly very God and very man, in the incomprehensible glory of his Father, to whom be all praise, honour, and glory, now and ever. Amen.

Laing IV, pp 192-4
{spelling modernised}

XXVI

Exhortation
to a Superintendent

[*This exhortation was given by Knox when John Spottiswoode was elected as Superintendent of Lothian on 9 March 1561. A much amended form of this exhortation is included in the 'Ordinal and Service Book of the Church of Scotland' (the 1954 and 1962 editions).*]

TAKE heed to thyself, and unto the Flock committed to thy charge; feed the same carefully, not as it were of compulsion, but of very love, which thou bearest to the Lord Jesus. Walk in simplicity and pureness of life, as it becometh the true servant and ambassador of the Lord Jesus. Usurp not dominion nor tyrannical empire over thy brethren. Be not discouraged in adversity, but lay before thyself the example of Prophets, Apostles, and of the Lord Jesus, who in their ministry sustained contradiction, contempt, persecution and death. Fear not to rebuke the world of sin, justice and judgment. If anything succeed prosperously in thy vocation, be not puffed up with pride; neither yet flatter thyself as that the good success proceeded from thy virtue, industry, or care: But let ever that sentence of the Apostle remain in thy heart; 'What has thou, which thou has not received? If thou hast received, why gloriest thou?' Comfort the afflicted, support the poor, and exhort others to support them. Be not solist [*ie* solicitous] for things of this life, but be fervent in prayer to God for increase of his Holy Spirit.

And finally, behave thyself in this holy vocation with such sobriety as God may be glorified in thy ministry: And so shall thou shortly obtain the victory, and shall receive the crown promised, when the Lord Jesus shall appear in his glory, whose Omnipotent Spirit assist thee and us unto the end. Amen.

Dickinson II, p 276 f

XXVII

KINGSHIP

[*These paragraphs are taken from a sermon preached by Knox on Sunday 19 August 1565 in the presence of King Henry, better known as Lord Darnley.*]

ISAIAH 26 verse 13: First the Prophet sayeth 'O Lord our God, other Lords besides thee have ruled us'.

FOR the better understanding of this complaint, and of the mind of the Prophet, we must first observe from whence all authority and dominion floweth; and secondly, to what end powers are appointed of God: The which two points being discussed, we shall the better understand what Lords, and what authority rules beside God, and who are they in whom God and his merciful presence rules.

The first is resolved to us by the words of the Apostle, saying, 'There is no power but of God.' David bringeth in the eternal God speaking to Judges and rulers saying, 'I have said, ye are Gods and the Sons of the most highest' (Psalm 82:6). And Solomon, in the person of God, affirmeth the same, saying, 'By me kings reign, and princes discern the things that are just' (Proverbs 8:15). Of which places it is evident, that it is neither birth, influence of stars, election of people, force of arms, nor, finally, what soever can be comprehended under the power of nature, that maketh the distinction betwixt the superior power and the inferior, or that doth establish the royal throne of kings; but it is the

110

only and perfect ordinance of God, who willeth his power, terror and Majesty in a part, to shine in the thrones of Kings, and in the faces of Judges, and that for the profit and comfort of man; so that who soever would study to deface the order of regiment that God hath established, and by his holy word allowed, and bring in such a confusion as no difference should be betwixt the upper powers and the subjects, doth nothing but evert and turn upside down the very throne of God, which he will to be fixed here upon earth, as in the end and cause of this ordinance more plainly shall appear; which is the second point we have to observe, for the better understanding of the Prophet's words and mind.

The end and cause then, why God printeth in the weak and feeble flesh of man this image of his own power and majesty, is not to puff up flesh in opinion of it self; neither yet that the heart of him that is exalted above others shall be lifted up by presumption and pride, and so despise others; but that he shall consider that he is appointed Lieutenant to one, whose eyes continually watch upon him, to see and examine how he behaveth himself in his office. Saint Paul in few words, declareth the end wherefore the sword is committed to the powers, saying, 'It is to the punishment of the wicked doers, and unto the praise of such as do well' (Romans 13:3,4).

Of which words, it is evident that the sword of God is not committed to the hand of man, to use as it pleaseth him, but only to punish vice and maintain virtue, that men may live in such society as before God is acceptable. And this is the very and only cause why God hath appointed powers in the earth. For such is the furious rage of man's corrupt nature that unless severe punishment were appointed, and put in execution upon malefactors, better it were that man should live among brute and wild beasts than among men.

* * *

The first thing then that God craveth of him that is called to the honour of a King is, The knowledge of his will revealed in his word.

The second is, An upright and willing mind to put in execution such things as God commandeth in his law, without declining either to the right or left hand.

Kings then have not an absolute power in their regiment what pleaseth them; but their power is limited by God's word: so that if they strike where God commandeth not, they are but murderers; and if they spare when God commandeth to strike, they and their throne are criminal and guilty of the wickedness that aboundeth upon the face of the earth, for lack of punishment.

O! if Kings and princes should consider what account shall be craved of them, as well of their ignorance and misknowledge of God's will, as for the neglecting of their office!

Laing VI, pp 235-8
{spelling modernised}

XXVIII

A PREACHER
RATHER THAN A WRITER

[The sermon preached before King Henry was the only one published by Knox in his lifetime. Here in the Preface he explains why.]

WONDER not, Christian Reader, that of all my study and travail within the Scriptures of God these twenty years, I have set forth nothing in exponing any portion of Scripture, except this only rude and indigest Sermon preached by me in the public audience of the Church in Edinburgh, the day and year above mentioned. That I did not in writ communicate my judgment upon the Scriptures, I have ever thought and yet think myself to have most just reason. For considering myself rather called of God to instruct the ignorant, comfort the sorrowful, confirm the weak, and rebuke the proud, by tongue and lively voice in these most corrupt days, than to compose books for the age to come, seeing that so much is written (and that by men of most singular condition), and yet so little well observed; I decreed to contain myself within the bonds of that vocation, whereunto I found myself especially called.

Laing VI, p 229
{spelling modernised}

XXIX

FASTING

[The following paragraphs are taken from 'The Order and Doctrine of the General Fast' prepared by Knox at the appointment of the General Assembly of 1565.]

OF Fasting, in the Scriptures we find two sorts; the one private, the other public. The private, is that which man or woman doeth in secret, and before their God, for such causes as their own conscience beareth record unto them. As David, during the time that his Son, which was begotten in adultery, was stricken with mortal sickness, fasted, wept, and lay upon the ground, because that in the sickness of the Child he did consider God's displeasure against him self; for the removing whereof he fasted, mourned, and prayed unto such time as he saw God's will fulfilled, by the awaytaking of the Child. Privately fasted Hannah, wife to Elkanah even in the very Solemn Feasts, during the time of her barrenness; for she wept and ate nothing, but in the bitterness of her heart she prayed unto the Lord; neither ceased she from sorrow and mourning, unto such time as Eli the high priest concurred with her in prayers, by whose mouth, after that he had heard her pitiful complaint, she received comfort.

Of this Fasting, speaketh our Master, Jesus Christ, in these words, 'When ye fast, be not sour as the Hypocrites, for they disfigure their faces that they seem unto men to fast; but thou, when thou fastest, anoint thy head and wash thy face, that thou seem not unto men to fast, but unto thy Father which seeth in secret, and will reward thee openly.' Of the same no doubt speaketh the Apostle, when that he sayeth, 'Defraud not one another, except it be with consent for a time, that ye may give yourselves to Fasting and prayer.'

To this private Fasting, which standeth chiefly in a temperate diet, and in pouring forth of our secret thoughts and necessities before God, can be prescribed no certain rule, certain time, nor certain ceremonies; but as the Causes and occasions why that exercise is used are divers (yea, so divers that seldom it is that many at once are moved with one cause), so are diet, time, together with all other circumstances, required to such Fasting, put in the liberty of them that use it.

* * *

The other kind of Fasting is public; so called, because that it is openly avowed, some times of a Realm, some times of a multitude, some times of a city, and some times of a meaner company, yea, some times of particular persons, and yet publicly used, and that for the wealth of a multitude. The Causes thereof are also divers; for sometimes the fear of enemies, some times the angry face of God punishing, some times his threatening to destroy, some times iniquity deprehended that rightly before was not considered, and some times the earnest zeal that some bear for preservation of God's people, for advancing of his glory, and performing of his work according to his promise, move men to public Fasting, confession of their sins, and solemn prayer, for defence against their enemies, recovering of God's favours, removing of his plagues, preservation of his people, and setting forward of that work, which he hath of his mercy promised to finish. _Laing VI, pp 394f_

XXX

CHRISTIAN JUSTICE

[The following paragraphs are taken from 'The Order and Doctrine of the General Fast' 1565.]

CHRISTIAN justice craveth more than Civil Laws.

It is not enough to justify us before God, that Civil Laws cannot accuse us. Nay, Brethren, the eyes of our God pierceth deeper than man's law can stretch. The law of man cannot convict the Earl, the Lord, the Baron, or Gentleman, for oppressing of the poor labourers of the ground; for his defence is ready, I may do with my own as best pleaseth me. The Merchant is just enough in his own conceit if before men he can not be convicted of theft and deceit. The Artificer and Craftsman thinketh himself free before God, albeit that he neither work sufficient stuff, nor yet sell for reasonable price: The world is evil (sayeth he), and how can men live if they do not as other do? And thus doth every man lean upon the iniquity of an other, and thinketh himself sufficiently excused when that he meeteth craft with craft, and repulseth back violence either with deceit or else with open injury. Let us be assured, dear brethren, that these be the sins which heretofore have provoked God, not only to plague, but also to destroy, and utterly overthrow strong realms and flourishing commonwealths.

* * *

To prescribe to every man his duty in particular, we can not, because we know not whereintill every man, and every estate particularly offendeth; but we must remit every estate, and every man in his vocation, to the examination of his own conscience; and that according as God commandeth in his whole Law, and as Christ Jesus requireth, that such as shall possess the Kingdom with him shall do; which is, 'Whatsoever (sayeth he) that ye would men should do unto you, do ye the like unto them.' By this rule, which the author of all equity, justice and policy hath established, send we the Earls, Lords, Barons, and Gentlemen to try their own consciences, whether they would be content that they should be entreated (if God had made them husbandmen and labourers of the ground) as they have entreated, and presently doth entreat, such as sometimes had a moderate and reasonable life under their predecessors.... And unto the same rule we send Judges, Lawyers, Merchants, Artificers, and finally, even the very labourers of the ground themselves, that every one in his vocation may try how justly, uprightly, and mercifully he dealeth with his Neighbour: And if he find his conscience accused by the former sentence of our Master, let him call for grace, that he may not only repent for the by past, but also amend in times to come; and so shall their Fasting and Prayers be acceptable unto God.

Laing VI, pp 412-414
{spelling modernised}

XXXI

A Painful Preacher

[In the following extract from a letter written in 1568 to a friend resident in England, Knox reflects on reactions to the 'First Blast' and on his ministry.]

BECAUSE I have the testimony of a good conscience, that in writing that Treatise, against which so many worldly men have stormed, and yet storm, I neither sought myself nor worldly promotion; and because, as yet, I have neither heard nor seen law nor Scripture to overthrow my grounds, I may appeal to a more indifferent judge than Doctor Jewell. I would most gladly pass through the course that God hath appointed to my labours, in meditation with my God, and giving thanks to his holy name, for that it hath pleased his mercy to make me not a lord-like Bishop, but a painful Preacher of his blessed Evangel; in the function whereof it hath pleased his Majesty for Christ his son's sake, to deliver me from the contradiction of more enemies than one or two; which maketh me the more slow and less careful to revenge by word or writ, whatever injury hath been done against me in my own particular. But if that men will not cease to impugn the truth, the faithful will pardon me if I offend such as for pleasure of flesh fear not to offend God. The defence and maintenance of superstitious trifles produced never better fruit in the end than I perceive is budding amongst you; schism, which no doubt is a forerunner of greater

118

desolation, unless there be speedy repentance. God comfort that dispersed little flock, amongst whom I once lived with quietness of conscience and contentment of heart; and amongst whom I would be content to end my days, if so it might stand with God's good pleasure. For, seeing it hath pleased his Majesty, above all men's expectation, to prosper that work for the performing whereof I left that company, I would even as gladly return to them, if they stood in need of my labours, as ever I was glad to be delivered from the rage of mine enemies. I can give you no reason that I should so desire, other than that my heart so thirsteth.

Laing VI, pp 558f
{spelling modernised}

XXXII

A Prayer
in Time of Trouble

[This prayer was written in 1566 just before Knox was compelled to flee from Edinburgh, but was not published until 1572.]

LORD Jesus, receive my Spirit, and put an end at thy good pleasure, to this my miserable life; for justice and truth are not to be found amongst the sons of men! John Knox, with deliberate mind to his God.

Be merciful unto me, O Lord, and call not into judgment my manifold sins; and chiefly those, whereof the world is not able to accuse me. In youth, mid age, and now, after many battles, I find nothing into me but vanity and corruption. For, in quietness I am negligent, in trouble impatient, tending to desperation; and in the mean state, I am so carried away with vain fantasies that, (alas), O Lord, they withdraw me from the presence of thy Majesty. Pride and ambition assault me on the one part, covetousness and malice trouble me on the other: briefly, O Lord, the affections of the flesh do almost suppress the operation of thy Spirit. I take thee, O Lord (who only knows the secrets of hearts) to record, that in none of the foresaid I do delight; but that with them I am troubled, and that sore against the desire of my inward man, which sobs for my corruption, and would repose in thy mercy alone. To the which I claim, and that in the promise that thou has made to all penitent sinners (of whose number I profess myself to be one) in the obedience and death of my only Saviour, our Lord Jesus Christ. In whom, by thy mere grace, I doubt not myself to be elected to eternal salvation, whereof thou has given unto me (unto me, O Lord, most wretched and unthankful creature) most assured signs. For being drowned in my ignorance, thou has given to me knowledge above the common sort of my brethren; my tongue has thou used to set forth thy glory, to oppugn idolatry, errors, and false doctrine. Thou has compelled me to fore-speak, as well deliverance to the afflicted, as destruction to certain inobedient; the performance whereof, not I alone but the very blind world has already seen. But above all, O Lord, thou, by the power of thy Holy Spirit, has sealed into my heart remission of my sins, which I acknowledge and confess my self to have received by the precious blood of Jesus Christ once shed; by whose perfect obedience I am assured my manifold rebellions are defaced, my grievous sins purged, and my soul made the tabernacle of thy godly Majesty. Thou, O Father of mercies, thy Son our Lord Jesus, my only Saviour, Mediator, and Advocate, and thy Holy Spirit, remaining in the same true faith; which is the only victory that overcometh the world.

To thee, therefore, O Lord, I commend my spirit; for I thirst to be resolved from this body of sin, and am assured that I shall rise again in glory, howsoever it be that the wicked, for a time, shall tread me, and others thy servants, under their feet. Be merciful, O Lord, unto the Kirk within this Realm; continue with it the light of thy Evangel; augment the number of true preachers; and let thy merciful providence look upon my desolate bedfellow, the fruit of her bosom, and my two dear children, Nathaniel and Eleazar. Now, Lord, put end to my misery!

Laing VI, pp 483 f
{spelling modernised}

BIBLIOGRAPHY
TO WORKS CITED IN PART 2

An answer to a great nomber of blasphemous cavillations written by an Anabaptist and adversarie to God's eternal predestination (Geneva 1560) (*Laing* V, 19-468).

History of the Reformation of religion within the realm of Scotland (London 1587) (*Dickinson* ed, 1949).

A Brief Sommarie of the Work by Balnaves on Justification (place and date of publication unknown) (*Laing* III, 5-28).

Heir is breiflie declarit in a Summe, according to the Holie Scriptures, what opinioun we Christians haif of the Lordis Supper, callit The Sacrament of the Bodie and Blude of our Savioure Jesus Chryst. Written in 1550 and annexed to other Works (*Laing* III, 73-75).

Memorial to the Privy Council (*Lorimer,* 267-274).

Letter to the Congregation of Berwick (*Lorimer,* 251-265).

Letter to Mrs Bowes (*Laing* III, 282-285).

A Declaratioun what trew Prayer is, how we suld Pray and for what we suld pray. Set furth be Johne Knox, Preacher of Godis holie word. (Rome [!] 1554) (*Laing* III, 83-109).

Letter to Marjory Bowes (*Laing* III, 394-395).

A godly letter sent too the faythfull in London, Newcastell, Barwycke, and to all the other within the realme off England that love the cominge of our Lorde Jesus by Jhon Knox (Rome [!] 1554) (*Laing* III, 165-216).

A Faythfull admonition made by John Knox unto the professours of Gods truthe in England, wherby thou mayest learne howe God wyll have his Churche exercised with troubles, and how he defendeth it in the same (Emden 1554) (*Laing* III, 257-330).

A notable and Comfortable exposition of M John Knoxes, upon the fourth of Mathew, concerning the tentations of Christ ... (London 1583) (*Laing* IV, 89-114).

A most wholsome counsell, how to behave ourselves in the myddes of thys wycked generation touching the daily exercise of Gods most holy and sacred worde (Wesel 1556) (*Laing* IV, 133-140).

The First Blast of the Trumpet against the monstrous regiment of women (Geneva 1558) (*Laing* IV, 363-420).

Supplication and exhortation to the nobilitie, estates, and communaltie of Scotland (Geneva 1558) (*Laing* IV, 523-538).

The form of prayers and ministration of the Sacrament, etc., used in the Englishe Congregation at Geneva: and approved, by the famous and godly learned man, John Calvyn (Geneva 1556) (*Laing* IV, 141-214).

A sermon preached by John Knox Minister of Christ Jesus in the Publique audience of the Church of Edenbrough, within the Realme of

Scotland, upon Sunday, the 19 of August 1565 (London 1566) (*Laing* VI, 391-428).

The Ordour and Doctrine of the General Faste, appointed be the Generall Assemblie of the Kirkes of Scotland halden at Edinburgh the 25 Day of December 1565 (Edinburgh 1566) (*Laing* VI, 391-428).

Letter to Mr John Wood (*Laing* VI, 558-559).

An Answer to a letter of a Jesuit named Tyrie, be Johne Knox (St Andrews 1572) (*Laing* VI, 479-514).

For a fuller list of Knox's writings see Ian Hazlett, 'A Working Bibliography of Writings by John Knox' in *Calviniana* X, pp 185-193. I acknowledge my great indebtedness to Dr Hazlett's work.

I also acknowledge the valuable help given by Mr Colin G McAlister in reading the proofs and checking references.